JAC...,

A Story of Everyday Life.

BY

SALOME HOCKING,

Author of " Norah Lang," " Granny's Hero," &c., &c.

London:

ANDREW CROMBIE, 119, SALISBURY SQUARE,
FLEET STREET, E.C.

"She was lying apparently lifeless on the ground, with a great cut on her forehead." See page 69.

Contents.

— ❧ —

JACKY.

A STORY OF EVERYDAY LIFE.

CHAPTER I.

EAVESDROPPING.

T was a dark, cold night, with a piercing wind and occasional showers of hail. It was a night that made any person who was so unfortunate as to be out think that a warm room and a blazing fire would be the acme of happiness.

Next to a warm room, in the estimation of most villagers, comes the village smithy. For though the shop may be of the rudest description, the fire there is generally of the brightest.

The smith's shop at the Great Louisa Mine is not lacking of this element of comfort on this particular evening, and, with the reader's permission, we will enter. A thing we may safely do, for its doors are hospitably open to all comers.

The smith has gone home, but the place is not unoccupied, for two miners are sitting in front of the fire eating their "crib." They are talking in low, earnest tones, and as the firelight flickers across their faces we can see that they are lit up with a kind of suppressed excitement. Let us listen to what the shorter and older of the two is saying,—

"I tell you I saw it as plain as anything. The water had run down, and there it was shining like silver, a great vein of solid tin. If we can only get that piece of ground our fortin' is made, Bob."

"Aye, aye, comrade. But won't the Cap'n suspect something when two experienced miners like you and me leave a good job and ask to take a piece of ground that has been worked out years and years ago?" And the man addressed as "Bob" looked anxiously into the other's face.

The one addressed as "Comrade" cut another thick slice from his "crib," and, holding it aloft between his finger and thumb, burst into a loud laugh, and, with a merry twinkle in his big blue eyes, answered,—

"I think my repytation will come in handy here, Bob. When I tell Cap'n what I want, he'll say aside to the clerk, 'The old fool is never satisfied unless he's working on his own hook. I really believe he'd rather work for sixpence a day less to be his own master.' And then he'll laugh and shake his head at me, and say, ' If there's any tin to be found you'll find it, Jan.' And then, after he's had his joke, he'll come to business, and the ground will be ours."

" Well, I hope so," answered Bob, anxiously, " for I could not bear to be disappointed now. But, come along, it is time for us to be going down." And taking up some tools they left the shop.

As soon as they were out of hearing, a man crept from behind an old barrel and some other rubbish that had been thrown into a corner by the side of the chimney, and as he stepped up to the fire to warm his hands, he chuckled to himself as if he were 'very much pleased about something, and said half aloud,—

" We'll see, my fine fellows, who will have that piece of ground, for if there's a fortin' to be made, why not mine, eh ? I'll see the Cap'n early Saturday morning. I'll not wait till he pays my wages, for it is always their turn to be paid before mine. I would go to-morrow, only I knaw the Cap'n will be away. I'm glad I slipped behind that barrel when I 'eard 'em comin'," and Nicholas Green laughed again, his low unmusical laugh.

He was a young man about twenty-five or six years

of age, with a pale, thin face, and small reddish brown eyes. His thin hair was also of a reddish tinge, and always looked as if it were damp, either with oil or perspiration. He had hidden some candles in the barrel in the earlier part of the day, and now had come in the evening when no one was about to take them away. Putting them in a bag, which he had brought for the purpose, he stepped out into the darkness.

As soon as the sound of his footsteps had died away, there was a movement on the forge from what had looked like an old jacket rolled up into a ball. Soon there was visible a pair of eyes which peered eagerly about the shop, then the owner of the eyes hastily shook off the old jacket, and sprang nimbly from the forge.

When we first catch sight of the little figure, with his pale innocent face, and high white forehead, we are filled with wonder that such a child should be away from home at that time of the evening; and above all places in the world, on a mine, where are open shafts in every direction, and where one false step would send a soul into eternity. But as he turns his face towards the fire, and we see the large hump on his back, the idea strikes us that he may not be quite so young as his face would indicate; and when he again turns toward us, with one eye shut, and the other nearly so, and a lurking smile of mischief on his pale face, we are at a loss to know what age this sprite really is.

Some time after, we learnt that he was fifteen, but that he had fallen from a tree when he was ten years old, and injured his spine, which not only entirely put a stop to his growth, but had in the formation of the hump on his back, detracted from the height he had already attained, and he was no taller than many a child of six. Being so small and with his childish innocent face, people forgot how old he really was, and still treated him as if he were a child. This he resented very much, although he took good care they should not know it, for while they thought of him as a child, he had all the better chance of learning their secrets, and of showing them that they were in his—the little hunchback's—power. And that was revenge worth scheming for.

When anything particularly pleased him, he always shut one eye, and rubbed his hands softly, and would then say, with a laugh that sounded innocent enough,

"Well done, little Jacky."

This boy was a strange mixture of innocence and cunning, good and evil; and we ask ourselves which, as he grows older, will predominate ?

As he snatches up his cap and leaves the shop, running with swift but sure feet in and out between tall barrows and deep shafts, like one to whom every inch of ground is familiar, let us follow him to his home, and see what kind of influence surrounds him there.

Not far from the mine stands a good-sized village or town, as some of the inhabitants ambitiously called it, which was named Treggonoweth. Now, this village boasted of one street, which was proudly named London Street, and was the pride and joy of all those who lived in it. To live in London Street was a passport to the best society in a certain circle, hence there was never an empty house there. But there were degrees of respectability, even in aristocratic London Street; for the nearer a man lived to the centre the more respectable he was considered to be. Thus the shoemaker thought himself two degrees higher in the social scale than the tinker, because he lived two doors further up the street; while the tailor drew his small form up proudly, and would not so much as look at the tinker and shoemaker, for did he not live three doors higher up than either? But the landlord at the "Golden Arms" looked down with complacent contempt on them all, for did not he live in the very centre, and was not his the most magnificent house in all London Street? This he always took care to let them know when there was any dispute, which there often was of an evening, as to who was the most respectable; and then he would wind up his remarks by saying,—

" I practise what I recommend you all to practise, and that is humility. Though above you, I hold out the right hand of fellowship to every man. I welcome each one of you to my house, whether he lives at the top or the bottom of the street. I welcome you *all.*" This was perfectly true, and he might also have added, " And each one has to pay me dearly for that welcome."

There were two other public-houses in Treggono-weth, but they had not the honour of being in London Street, and hence were not nearly so popular.

The " Golden Arms " wore its most inviting aspect on the evening of which we have been writing. All the front of the house was well lit up, and a blazing fire might be seen through the uncurtained windows. Through the open door issued the sounds of a fiddle and snatches of song; and every now and then huge bursts of laughter might be heard. It was not very late in the evening, and the men were in the jolly stage. The quarrelsome stage would come later on, and then the landlord would shut the door and draw

the curtains across the windows. He did not mind
a little quarrelling, because it made them thirsty, so
he shut his ears to the noise and didn't even object
to a fight, so long as they were content with damag-
ing each others' faces and forms. But when they
began to smash his pictures and glasses, he would
call in his servant, a big, powerful fellow, who
walked in among them, administering a cuff here
and there with perfect good will. When peace was
restored, drinks would be called for all round, but as
soon as any one began to hiccough,—

"Cleaned out, old boy; pay you to-morrow," and
credit was asked for instead of money being laid
down for the drinks, the smile of good nature left the
landlord's face, and Bill, in answer to a wink from
his master, would take off his jacket and square for
action. Those who were not too drunk took the
hint and staggered out; and those who were, would
be helped out by Bill, some of them receiving a kick
by way of good night. If any of them should happen
to remember this treatment the next day, and com-
plain of it to the landlord, he would side with them,
and say that it was no wish of his that any gentleman
should be roughly treated who came to his house.
He would offer them the only satisfaction that lay in
his power, and that was that any gentleman should

give Bill the thrashing which he no doubt deserved. The sight of Bill's big, brawny figure in the doorway, in answer to his master's call, generally extinguished all desire for satisfaction, and the complainant would, with forced hilarity, call for a drink "for good old Bill, who would perhaps favour them with a song." Bill would grin at the request, and comply, being equally ready to sing or fight at a minute's notice.

It was just outside this house that Jacky Williams stopped on his way home through London Street; and putting his fingers to his mouth, he gave a long, shrill whistle.

CHAPTER II.

JACKY'S PLANS.

S the whistle penetrated to the bar, a boy slipped from behind the counter, and joined Jacky in the street. This boy was the landlord's eldest son.

"Hallo, little hunchie, 'ow are 'ee shinin'?" were his first words; and then, lowering his harsh tones to a whisper, he asked, "Have 'ee got they cigars and things?"

"Yes, here they are," answered Jacky, as he took a small parcel from his pocket, and gave the other.

"That's the ticket, my lad. Now come in, and 'ave a warmer. I'm jest gòin' to make up some prime 'ot drinks for some of the old duffers, and I'll make one for you. Come along."

"I can't stay now, for I am later than usual, and mother will be anxious about me; but I'll come in to-morrow evening, if you like."

"Jist the very thing I was wantin'. The guvnor's goin' away, and there will be a lot of people in to-morrow night on their way home from market; so you'll be able to 'elp me."

"All right; good night, Sol," and Jacky moved on again.

He did not go much further in London Street, but turned down an opening which led into a narrow lane. After walking a few minutes, he crossed a road by the side of which stood two cottages. The gardens attached to those cottages were separated from each other by a row of well-pruned thorns. Opening the lower gate, and walking with quick steps through the garden, Jacky lifted the latch, and entered the house.

By the fire, knitting, sat a stout, rosy, comely-looking woman, between forty and fifty years of age. This was Jacky's mother, who greeted him with a pleasant smile, and asked him where he had been so long?

Seated at the table, bending over a book, was a young girl of about twenty years. She looked up when Jacky entered, disclosing to view a rather pale face, with large, dreamy grey eyes, and, after nodding at him with an absent kind of smile, she again fixed her gaze on her book. This was Harriet, or Hattie Williams, Jacky's only sister. She was assistant mistress at the Board School, and had received a good sound education, of which her father was very proud. He would often say to his friends, " I am not much of a grammararian myself, but my girl can talk grammar enough for us both ; and, as for readin', you never knew anyone that had read so many books! "

Jacky sometimes wished that his sister was not so fond of reading, for then he thought she might take more interest in him ; for Hattie Williams lived in a world of her own creation, and books were her only companions. She knew more about what had happened in the Middle Ages than of what was happening around her in her own day. Her mind was stored with old Greek tales, ballads, and legends, with poetry of all ages, and romances that had long ago gone out of date. Of modern fiction she had read but little, for she had taken most of her books from the old schoolmaster's library. He took great interest in her ; but sometimes, when he saw how greedily she devoured a book, and how real the persons there represented seemed to her, he would shake his head, and say,—

" She can't go on always like this. The awakening will come some day. God grant that it may not be a sad one! "

As he looked at his sister's bent head that evening, Jacky thought, " I wonder if she would care if she knew what I have heard to-night, and what

I mean to do? Would she think it wrong to do evil that good might come? But what's the use of bothering? She doesn't care what I do; and it's not much of a trick any way. Ah, ah! Nick Green, the little Hunchie, as you always call him, is a match for you any day." And shutting one eye, he chuckled in his own peculiar way.

"What are you laughing about, Jacky?" asked his mother, laying her hand fondly on his head.

Jacky looked up with a start and a slight blush, then answered quickly, "Oh, nothing of any consequence;" and then, as if to turn the conversation, he asked, "Do you think it is possible for good to come out of evil, mother?"

"Well, I'm sure I don't know," answered Mrs. Williams, meditatively. And then, as a bright thought struck her, she said, "I suppose there can, for everything is possible with God. There, I wish your father had been here, he wouldn't be able to say *then* that I can't argue," and Mrs. Williams rattled her needles with a satisfied click.

Jacky laughed, and said, in amused tones, as if he were speaking to someone younger than himself,—

"Father doesn't know how clever you really are, mother dear."

"I believe you are right, Jacky," answered Mrs. Williams, seriously; "for he always says I can't argue a question, when I'm sure I always beat him. For he says nearly every time, 'It's no use my saying any more, for you will have your own way.' So that shows that I can hold out longer than he can."

"So you can, mother; and you always have the last word," said Jacky, mischievously.

"Well, why shouldn't I? One word is as good as another, and a little better if it's the last one. Now, there's your father, always botherin' his head over one passage of Scripture or another! What's the use of it, John?" says I, "we shan't get to heaven any easier or sooner for worritin' about it. Now, I never worrit about things, for it is sure to end all right, if *we* only wait long enough."

After delivering this comfortable piece of philosophy, Mrs. Williams folded up her knitting, and rose to get her husband's supper.

Not long after, John Williams came home, and we find that he is the one addressed as "comrade," whom we saw at the smith's shop. He had a kind, good-humoured, sensible face, and was evidently very fond of home and his children. But as he talked to his daughter, and asked her about what she was reading, it was manifest that his pride was centred in her rather than in his son. Jacky knew this, and though his father had always treated him with the most indulgent fondness, trying to make up in kindness for the great affliction that had fallen upon him, he resented it with great bitterness, and vowed that his father should one day alter his opinion.

Jacky had no confidant, for though he loved and respected his father, he was too proud to open his heart to one who pitied more than he admired him. For Jacky, like many another very little person, was intensely vain and proud, and did not like to be pitied, but wanted to be treated by men as an equal. As for his mother, he would never think of making a confidant of her, for to tell the truth, Jacky considered her inferior in intellect to himself, and generally treated her with the indulgent fondness of an elder brother. But apart from all this, there was no one in the wide world that he loved as he did his mother, for from her only did he receive the admiration which his vanity craved. She considered him the smartest boy in creation, and in her happy way of ignoring trouble, never took any notice of the deformity which seemed so pitiful in the eyes of other people. Jacky knew this also, and in her presence he almost forgot the deformity himself, and for *that* he worshipped her.

In his sister he considered that he had an equal, and would have taken her into his confidence had she given him the least encouragement, but living always with her books she forgot that there were people in the world with wants that she could supply. It never struck her that her life was not given her to be wasted in dreamland. Thus the only one who might have influenced Jacky for good was a dreamer, and saw not her opportunity; and he went on his way without check or hindrance.

The next evening, according to promise, Jacky was at the " Golden Arms " in good time, and after trying one of Sol's cigars, and gravely telling him that it was a "fragrant weed," Jacky took his place inside the bar to help Sol serve the customers who were dropping in. Every now and then he would slip out and look into the room where the men were seated, and then come back again. When he saw Nicholas Green coming towards the bar he slipped on the floor, muttering something about searching for a bottle of brandy. As soon as Green had left, he got up and asked quietly,—

" What does Nicky Green want ?"

" He wants me to mix him a good stiff glass of

brandy-grog; but I can't stay, for I must go down in the cellar for a bottle of father's prime old wine against Lawyer Benney comes, for he won't drink anything else. You know how to mix grog. You must make it strong of the water, and put plenty of sugar, and use the dark brandy.· That'll colour it up, and make it look strong, and I'll take the extra profit for my own self. I can cook the guv'nor if he is stingy." And with a coarse laugh the landlord's son moved off.

As soon as his back was turned, Jacky half filled the glass with strong whisky, and placing a few drops of the dark coloured brandy to make it the right colour, he put in sugar, and filled the glass with boiling water, and sent it in by Bill. In a short time Bill was back again with the glass to have it re-filled, for Nicholas Green had said it was the best grog he ever tasted in his life. Jacky turned his back towards Bill, while he put the whisky and brandy in the glass, and mixing it as before the grog was again taken to Green.

Several times that evening was that glass re-filled, but not always by Jacky, for when he heard Green singing " Jolly boys are we," he knew that what he had planned had come to pass, for Nicholas Green never sang unless he was drunk, and those who

C

heard him said they did not wonder at it, for no man in his right senses with a voice like that would attempt to sing.

Having helped the landlord's son in order to serve his own purpose, and that purpose being completed, Jacky had no intention of rendering him any further assistance, and saying good-night, and taking no notice of the hints about "deserting a fellow in the very thick of the business," Jacky went home. He had his plan already matured for the next morning to keep Green from seeing the Captain until after his father had been paid and the ground taken, for what he had done that evening was only a part of the scheme. But the other part of the plan was accomplished without his aid, and in a way that he had not bargained for.

CHAPTER III.

"Perhaps they Won't Have Me in Heaven."

ICHOLAS GREEN was one of those who required Bill's help to find the door that night, and being rather restive under that individual's not too gentle hands, he was helped out with rather more force than Bill usually expended on his master's customers; and slipping on the doorstep he fell, his head coming in contact with an old sharp iron scraper. It was a fearful cut which he received across the back of his head, but he soon got up again and staggered home.

What an awful sight he was for his poor old widowed mother to see, coming into the house at midnight. Staggering in with uncertain steps, and half-shut eyes, muttering curses in maudlin tones, his head lolling from side to side, exposing to view the wound at the back, he was a sight fearful enough to cause a shudder in the heart of a strong man. What then must have been the feelings of that poor mother, there in the house alone, an old and feeble woman! God pity and help her, for no one else is near.

Could Jacky Williams have seen that poor widowed mother, with white face and shaking hands, trying to wash the blood from her son's head, and bind up the wound ; and could he have heard the muttered curses and seen the ill-natured kicks with which those services were received, methinks he would hardly have cared to again use the evil instrument *drink*, that good might come. And to do him justice, when he heard on the Saturday that Nicholas Green had fallen and injured his head, and was unable to get out of bed, his conscience gave him no rest, and he was greatly alarmed and ashamed at the part he had played. But when he saw Green a few days after with his head bound up, and asked him in timid tones how he was, and received the surly answer, " What's that to you, Hunchie ? You'd better mind your own business," remorse died out of his heart, and instead of being sorry for what he had done, he chuckled to himself as he thought how neatly he had outwitted Nicholas Green.

But when he heard his father telling his mother a month later that "Nicky Green " had taken the piece of ground adjoining theirs, and was going to try his hand at being " tributer," he ceased to chuckle, and wondered what Nicky's motive was for doing that ?

Making up his mind that he would find out, Jacky again made use of his friend Sol, and helped him behind the bar, evening after evening; but it was of no use, for Nicholas Green never once in all that time entered the "Golden Arms." Knowing that he had a secret which he wished to keep from everyone, and knowing, too, the old saying that "when the liquor is in the wit is out," he wisely resolved to eschew the "Golden Arms," and turn teetotaler for the nonce.

Nicholas Green had full faith in John Williams' discriminating power for finding tin, and though he did not know tin from "black-jack" himself, he confidently expected to make his "fortin." So, being not too fond of hard work, he dug the ground that was easiest to be got at, for if tin were there—he argued, and of that he was certain, for did not John Williams say he saw it—why, it was as likely to be in the loose ground as in the hard. What was his horror at the end of the month when he went to receive his wages, to find that instead of having any money to take up, he was in debt; there not being tin enough in the pile he had sent to surface to pay for stamping and cost of cleaning. His disappointment was great, but his anger was greater, and vowing to himself as he walked moodily homeward, with his hands in his empty pockets, that John Williams should suffer for it if he had deceived him, he began to wonder how he should find out. Then remembering the complacent smile that he had seen on John Williams' face as he left the Counting House, he decided that he must have had a good "pay-day," and to have had that, he must have found plenty of tin.

That evening he startled his mother by bringing down his fist on the table with a bang, and saying in exulting tones,—

"I'm blowed if that isn't the very thing. I can make her do anything for me."

"What is it you want me to do, my son?" asked his poor old mother, timidly.

"I want you to make a jug of cocoa instead of tea for my supper. You will, won't you?" he asked artfully, in wheedling tones.

"Of course I will," answered the mother, unsuspiciously, glad to see the lowering cloud lifted from his face.

Jacky puzzled his head many times over Green's continued absence from the "Golden Arms," and wondered what mischief he was working out so quietly; for Jacky felt sure that he had some purpose in taking the piece of ground next to his father's.

It was not, however, until another month had slipped by, and he heard his father talking to Bob, his comrade, when they met to share their wages, that he received a clue to the mystery.

" I can't understand it at all," said John. " We have dug quite as much stuff as we did last month, if not more ; and here we haven't half as much wages. I can't see through it."

" Neither can I," answered Bob. " The costs haven't been more this month, either; but didn't the Cap'n say that there was not nearly so much tin in our work ? "

" Yes, he said so; but I could swear that there was a heap more tin in this month's work than last."

" Well, it is no use worrying ; better luck next time," said Bob, as he pocketed his share of the wages.

As the reader will meet Bob again in these pages, we think he ought to be introduced in a more fitting manner. We forbore to give a description of him when we saw him at the smith's shop, for though he looked picturesque enough in his dirty underground rags, he would not have liked it ; for Bob, apart from his work, was the picture of cleanliness, and was always well dressed. He stood five feet eleven inches in his stockings, and with his broad shoulders and

muscular frame, looked built for strength. Bob was
not handsome, for his cheek-bones were too high, and
his chin rather too aggressive for beauty, but the deep
set brown eyes were decidedly handsome and lit up
his otherwise plain face. Such was Bob or Robert
Trethewey at twenty-eight.

Jacky had listened attentively to the conversation
between his father and Bob, and came to the conclu-
sion that the mystery about the wages lay with Nicky
Green ; but how to be certain, that was the trouble.
At first he thought of going underground the following Monday, and watching Green at work ; but then
remembering that the latter could take nothing from
his father while he and Bob were there, he dismissed
that plan as useless. Besides, he argued, what
trickery was done, must be done on the surface, for
his father would detect it if his work were disturbed.
Then, if that were so, Green must have a confederate
on the surface who helped him. The first thing to
find out was, who haled the stuff from underground,
and whose hands it next passed through ; and to find
that out, Jacky resolved to spend the next Monday
at the mine. This he could easily do, as he had a
holiday at school.

Having settled his plans to his own satisfaction,
Jacky took his violin, and laying his pale cheek on it

with a caressing touch, he began to play with such taste and feeling as only one who had a love for music could do. Looking at him, with his yellow hair thrown back from his high forehead, and his blue eyes opened wide, and the child-like innocent look more marked than usual; no one would think him capable of hatching schemes or harbouring feelings of revenge. But the musical side of his nature was uppermost that evening, and when that was the case, Jacky was always at his best.

After he had played and sang in soft low tones, that beautiful little hymn,—

" I've heard of a world of beauty,
Where there is no gloomy night,
Where love is the mainspring of duty,
And God is the fountain of light,"

Mrs. Williams wiped her eyes, and said in low fond tones,—

" I don't fancy that I should think the singing in heaven perfect, unless I heard my Jacky's voice there."

Jacky stirred a little uneasily, and said with a short laugh, " Perhaps they won't have me in heaven, mother."

" Not have you there! Why, you scarcely ever did anything wicked in your life. And if you had,

God would not keep you out of heaven after afflicting you as He has done," answered his mother, in tones of certainty.

Jacky forgot the strange fact of his mother's alluding to his deformity, in the delight with which he listened to her words. He always thought that he had brought his affliction on himself, for his father warned him several times not to climb the tall fir-tree at the back of their house, but he had disregarded the warning and was severely punished as he believed for his disobedience; but if his mother were right, why then it was an affliction from God, and he (Jack) was in no way responsible for it. Hitherto he had not complained, for no one was to blame but himself, but if it were otherwise, why then, as his mother said, he deserved heaven, and so need not suffer any remorse for some doubtful things which he had done at the " Golden Arms."

Strange reasoning, and coming from a strange mind. Poor Jacky! his conscience was growing as crooked as his back.

CHAPTER IV.

Jacky Finds a Clue.

ONDAY was a warm, balmy day. The wind which but a few days before had roared past with all its mighty and destructive force, twisting off limbs from trees and blowing roots out of the ground, was now toned down to a gentle breeze, which blew on one's face with a soft caressing touch, and lingered among the tree-tops with gentle whispers. It was a day that reminded one of the coming spring. The sun shone with genial warmth, and the bees came out of their hives, and flew around with cheerful hum, while the birds sang their sweetest songs, and all the earth looked glad.

Jacky took but little notice of the weather, he was too much wrapped up in his own thoughts and plans, as he walked towards the Great Louisa Mine that morning. He was not driven away by the old " tin dresser " as soon as he came in sight, as most of the boys were, for Jacky never meddled with anything, or got into mischief, so he was free to go where he liked. Most of the men pitied him and had a kind word for the little pale faced child, as they thought him; but others thoughtlessly made fun of him, of whom Nicky Green was one. They little knew when they were making their coarse jokes at Jacky's expense, what bitter passions they roused in his small frame, nor what schemes of revenge were seething in his active brain, as he passed by them without a word.

Jacky knew the shaft from which his father and Nicky Green's work would be drawn, and standing at a little distance from the spot, he watched the two men at work. He saw one man let down an empty kibble and pull up a full one, while the other wheeled the stuff away to a pile. Walking up to the man as he emptied his wheelbarrow, he asked,—

" Is there tin in that stuff ? "

" Yes, there's tin in it, little man, but I s'poase you can't see any. This is your father's pile, and that's Nicky Green's over there. It'll be a haccident if there is any tin in his, for he doant knaw tin from turmuts," and the man laughed, as if proud of his joke.

" No trickery here," thought Jacky. A minute after he asked—

" What's Kit Turner doing ? "

" She's kinder sorting it out, and putting away the best work to a pile. You see they have to pay for cleanin' the tin, so it's a pity to waste time over the addle, so she picks it over and throws the poor stuff away. She would knaw tin with her eyes shut. She can smell it, I reckon," and with another laugh the man went back with his empty wheelbarrow.

"A woman at the bottom of this mischief as usual," reflected Jacky, as he pretended to be looking at the stones of tin. "It is easy enough for her to throw the best work on Nicky Green's pile. I must talk to her a little bit," and sauntering towards the girl, Jacky sat down on a large rock, and said,—

"Much tin in the work, Kitty?"

"Some of it is pretty good, and some of it is very poor," answered the girl, without looking up.

"Nicky Green's is good, I suppose; he is such a clever miner."

The girl looked up quickly, with alarm written on her rather good-looking face; but seeing how innocent and childlike Jacky looked, she laughed carelessly, and said,—

"Not better than the others, you poor baby."

Jacky had seen all through his half-closed, eyes, and smiling, he thought,—

"That string will work when I want to pull it." And then taking up an old hammer that was lying near, he commenced to break some of the stones from

Nicky Green's pile. Jacky had picked up a good bit of knowledge about mining during the many holidays he had spent at the Great Louisa, and he had also heard his father and Bob Trethewey have many long talks on the subject, so that he was quite miner enough to know that Nicky Green's pile was "good work." Then crossing over to his father's pile, he broke several of the stones, but soon saw that there was very little tin in them.

Having seen enough to satisfy him, Jacky sauntered home, and seating himself in front of the fire, his favourite position when he wanted to think, he asked himself what inducement Nicky Green could have held out to this girl to make her act such a dishonest part. Kit Turner had always been considered quiet and honest, and Jacky felt sure that she was not doing it for money.

"They will meet one of these dark evenings, and then the girl is sure to talk about it, for her conscience won't be easy. I must hear what she says," thought Jacky. "Nicky Green will not want anyone to see them together for fear of suspicion, so they will meet when there aren't many people about. To-night, perhaps, as there is nothing doing at church or chapel. I will go up to Kit Turner's house about eight o'clock and watch."

At a quarter to eight that evening, Jacky quietly slipped out of the house. He had his mother's goloshes in his pockets, and when he entered the dark lane outside Kitty Turner's home, he put them on over his shoes and waited. He had not long to wait, for soon he heard the gate click, and peering out from behind the bush where he was hiding, he saw a dark figure come out at the gate, and then disappear in the darkness. Following quickly and noiselessly after, Jacky was soon close behind her, and when she stopped by a gap in the hedge, he stopped also. They waited there for what seemed a very long time to Jacky, and once or twice he resolved to go home, but curiosity and revenge kept him there.

" I am not the only one who is tired, I reckon," thought Jacky, as he heard a low sob from the motionless figure by the gap.

It was just when the figure had turned and taken a step down the road, as if to go home, that someone sprang through the gap into the road, and said, interrogatively, in a low voice,—

" Kit ? "

" Yes, Nicky, I'm here," was the answer in quaver-ing tones. " I thought you wasn't comin', you are so late."

"I couldn't get away before. But what are you crying for? Just like a great baby."

"Oh, Nick, I am so miserable. I haven't any peace, day or night. Whatever would my father say if he knew all?" answered the girl, with what sounded to Jacky like a burst of weeping.

"Now, once for all, let us end this," answered the man, roughly. "Either you are going to stick to me and do as I tell you, or I shall marry Angelina Drew, that is all."

"You daren't," answered the girl, in passionate tones.

"Daren't I?" he asked, mimicing her. "I dare do a lot more than you think."

Then there were some words which Jacky could not hear. The next words he heard were spoken in coaxing tones, and seemed to be in answer to something the girl had said.

"We must end this nonsense. I'd rather marry you than any other girl, Kit; and if you do as well as you did last month we shall soon be able to leave this country, and when we get to America you shall be as honest as you like. What do you say? Will you do what I want, like a sensible girl, and not bother my life out, or must I marry Angelina Drew?"

" I'll kill you both if you do," answered the girl, fiercely. And then, breaking down, she cried, piteously, "Oh, Nicky, I am in your power, I know; but if you have a spark of pity for the girl who loves you better than her own self, don't make me run my soul into more sin."

" Sin! Why there is no sin in it, you fool. Haven't I heard you laugh to hear your father tell how his father used to smuggle goods, and haven't you said that you didn't think it was very wrong to cheat the revenue? Why, this is just the same thing, and you'll be as ready to laugh over this little trick when we get to America. So cheer up, and be your own fascinatin' little self."

" Am I fascinatin'?" asked the girl, in pleased tones. " I'll do anything for you if you'll be nice, like you are now."

And Jacky heard the sound of a kiss, and then they moved on out of hearing.

" Humph," muttered Jacky, "what a simpleton she must be to let that ugly lout twist her around his finger in that fashion. He knows how to lay on the ' soft sawder,' any way."

Then, thinking that he had heard enough, he took a short cut across the fields, and was soon home again.

For several days Jacky was puzzled to know what use to make of his knowledge. He did not want to take any one into his confidence until the thing was accomplished. He wanted to show his father and Bob that the mystery which they had failed to find out had been solved by little despised Jacky. But, how to bring it about, that was the trouble. At last he decided to begin with the girl first. He would work on her fears.

Jacky did not intend to expose the girl, but to frighten her into being honest, and to have a sword which he could hold over Nicky Green's head.

"That will be sweet revenge," thought Jacky, "and will make the insolent fellow as mild as milk. For all the insulting remarks he has made about me I will take my pay now, and Nicky Green shall fare sumptuously on humble pie," and Jacky shut one eye and chuckled over his coming triumph.

CHAPTER V.

THE MYSTERY SOLVED.

FOLLOWING up this plan, Jacky walked to the Great Louisa Mine early one afternoon, about a week after the events narrated in our last chapter; and seating himself near where Kitty Turner was at work, he said, quietly,—

"How much are you thinking to make Nicky Green's wages this month, Kit?"

The girl was frightened, and began to tremble, but again on looking at Jacky's face she seemed reassured, and answered, quietly:

"I don't make Nicky's, he makes them hisself."

"Not a bit of it, my dear," said Jacky patronisingly. "You and I both know that it is my father, and Bob Tretheway who make Nicky Green's wages, though I expect that you receive all the thanks for it. Quite right, too, for I fancy that father and Bob don't do their share of the business quite as willingly as you do, eh, Kitty?"

"Who—what do you mean?" asked the girl in tones of terror, her face white with fear.

"Mean! Why that Nicky Green will marry you instead of Angelina Drew, if you go on stealing from my father and Bob. I always thought that you was an honest girl, Kit, but I know differently now. What do you think your father would say if he knew?"

"It would break his heart," answered the girl, weeping bitterly. "I wish I was dead. If I could only die now before he knew *all*," and covering her face, she rocked to and fro in an abandonment of misery.

"Don't cry like that," said Jacky, touched by the girl's great grief. "I'm not going to expose you, if you will do as I tell you."

"What is that? Don't ask me to do anything wicked, for I will not run my soul into more sin, I will go to prison first. Oh, Lord, help me!" said the girl, hysterically.

"I am not going to ask you to do anything wicked, I want you to stop *being* wicked. You must promise to put all my father's tin back to his pile, that is, all that he has sent up this month, and to work honestly for the future.

"I will, I will, oh, so gladly," answered the girl, drying her eyes. "And I will tell Nicky that he has been found out, and then he can't blame me."

"Yes; tell him that the 'little hunchie' knows

all about it, and that for the future he had better treat me with respect, or some of his deeds will see daylight. Tell him also that I was in the smith's shop, and heard what he said, and saw him put the candles he had 'cribbed' in his bag. When you have told him all this, give me his answer," and thrusting his hands in his pockets, Jacky was strutting away, when the girl said eagerly :

"I will see him before I leave the mine. I shan't see him this week if I don't do that, for he is afternoon core. Come here to-morrow, and I'll tell you what he says."

"Please yourself," answered Jacky, and then he added kindly, "Don't fret too much about it, Kit. I am sure that you would rather do what was right if it had not been for Nicky. He is a bad bargain, and I would give him up if I were you. Good-bye, be a good girl." And Jacky walked away.

That same afternoon Nicholas Green, John Williams, and Bob Trethewey were all busy at work. Not far from them was a party of men, who were "driving," to use the miners' phrase, in expectation of cutting water. This was being done, that that part of the mine might be pumped dry, so as to assist further explorations.

For some days the men had been expecting to cut

through the solid ground, and many times when a
little jet of water had trickled down they had raised
the shout of "water," and all the men working in the
adjoining cross-cuts and levels had left their work
and dashed to the footway or ladders. The false
alarm had been sounded so many times, that the
men working near were getting careless, and would
drop their tools grumblingly and walk leisurely to
the ladders; and many bitter speeches were hurled
at the men who had raised the cry. But when the
time came that the ground was really pierced through
and they could hear the roar of the water as it rushed
through the small hole which they had made, there
was no mistaking then.

Many sounds had been mistaken for water, but they
could not mistake *that* sound for anything else; so
running like men panic-stricken, they shouted in
hoarse tones as they rushed past, "Water! water!
run for your lives!"

It did not strike them that they had shouted such
words a dozen times before, when there was no
danger. The roaring of the water was in their ears,
and death was behind them, and no thought entered
their minds that the others had not the same fear
and knew not that danger was so nigh. Never
dreaming but that their comrades were following

after, they climbed the ladders with a speed they had never before equalled.

"There they are, shouting 'water' again," said Bob Trethewey, as he dropped his shovel a little impatiently. "Come, John, the real cry must come some time, and this may be the one."

"All right," answered John Williams, quietly; "I'll follow you," and they walked leisurely on.

They had not gone many steps before Bob's quick ears caught the sound of the water, and with a cry of fear he shouted—"Run for your life, John! I can hear it roaring like thunder!"

With quick, heavy pants, like men in pain, they passed as rapidly through the level as their stooping postures would allow. Not a minute was to be lost, for they could feel the water creeping around their feet, and a little further on it was up to their knees, and by the time they had got to the mouth of the level, which opened on to the plat where the ladders stood, it was up to their waists. And then, all at once, they heard a crash as if all the ground were falling about them. They knew the sound. The water had broken down the last piece of wall which had been keeping it back, and on it rushed through the hollowed and echoing ground, like the roar of ten thousand thunders.

The two men dashed through the water, which was now nearly up to their necks, and Bob, being ahead, caught the ladder first; but here the heroism of the homely fellow spoke out. Stepping aside, but still holding by the ladder, he said, "You go first, John."

Knowing that there was no time for hesitation John did as he was bidden, but in putting his foot on the ladder it slipped through and twisted right round, causing him the most acute pain. With a heavy groan he reeled to one side, and said, with a gasp,—

"Save yourself, Bob; I've sprained my ankle, and can't climb those ladders to save my life."

"Get on my back, and hold tight. Quick, or we shall be lost!" And in another second the brave fellow was climbing the ladders with John Williams on his back.

He was no light weight, but death was at their heels, and it was a race for life. Who would win? As John heard his companion's heavy straining breath he had to shut his teeth hard to refrain from groaning aloud, and great drops of sweat broke over his face as he thought of what would be their fate if Bob's strength failed him. He could hear the roar of the water, and he knew by the sound that it was still rising rapidly in the shaft.

The strain on Bob's muscles was great, and his breath came with heavy wheezing gasps, but still he plodded on, though his steps were getting slower and slower, and then they ceased altogether. But it was only for a minute, while he rested against the ladder, and then he laboured on again.

Perhaps it would be hard to tell which suffered the most acute pain, Bob Trethewey physically, or John Williams mentally; and when they reached the plat where the " skip " was, and John knew that they were comparatively safe, he wept like a little child.

But not so Bob, one last effort he made, and lifted John into the " skip," and then fell down exhausted by the side. John saw that he was incapable of further action, and, raising himself on his knees, he reached over and pulled him into their ark of safety, and then gave the signal for them to be drawn to the surface.

Those who have never been underground when danger was nigh, never known what it is to feel that the next minute your body might be lifeless clay, while your soul was drifting into the unknown, cannot realise with what feelings of thankfulness and joy John Williams and Bob Trethewey hailed the daylight, nor with what a close grasp they clasped the hands of the men who helped them on firm ground.

"All the men are up now, I believe," said the Captain, as his gaze wandered over the little group of miners standing by the shaft.

The men looked around at each other as the Captain spoke, and then one said hurriedly, "Where's Nicky Green? Has anyone seen him?"

Each man looked at his neighbour, but no one spoke.

"What!" said the Captain. "Do you mean to say he has not come up?" A silence as of death fell on the men. "God help him then," said the Captain in awe-struck tones, "for man cannot."

After awhile he spoke again, and said, "It's no use your staying here, men, you can do no good. Go home and thank God that death has passed you by, and that you are still given time to repent of your sins." And then he turned to help John Williams into the trap which had been sent for to convey him home.

CHAPTER VI.

"My Plans are all Useless."

AFTER walking into the engine-house, to give some directions to the engine-driver, Captain Lobb came back to where the men were still standing by the shaft, and said, kindly,—

"I respect your feelings, men. I know you feel loth to leave your comrade down there in those dark waters alone, but as I said before, you can do no good. I have given instructions for full steam to be put on, but it will be two days or more, before the place can be pumped dry enough for you to search for all that remains of Nicholas Green. Let us hope that when he saw his danger, he, like the thief on the cross, was pardoned at the eleventh hour."

"It's not him we are thinking so much about, Cap'n. It's his poor old mother. Who will tell her?" answered one of the men in pitiful tones.

"Ah! I had quite forgotten her," said the Captain, with a start.

"It's a hard job for whoever takes it. I'd rather work a doubler, tired as I am, than I'd be the one," said a strong stalwart fellow, who had caused plenty of suffering to his family in his day, by his intemperate habits; but who, when sober, shrank from witnessing any kind of suffering.

"Perhaps as Captain and Ned Trethewey are Christians, one of them would be the most fitting to go. They would know just what to say to her better than we should," said another insinuatingly.

"Whether you meant it or not you have paid one of the greatest tributes to Christianity that you could pay," said Captain Lobb earnestly, "for it shows that you think religion fits a man for the most delicate and difficult tasks. Fits him to break grievous news gently, and to pour consolation into the heart of a widow whose only son is dead. My men, religion not only helps a man to *break* ill news gently, but it enables him to *bear* it manfully when it comes to his share. You all know that touching story of Christ restoring to life the only son of the widow of Nain : let me tell you that the same Divine kindness has been guarding you amidst danger to-day, and has followed you all your lives. Think it well over, men. Let the sudden death of your comrade be a warning to you. 'For in such an hour as ye think not, the Son of Man cometh.'" Then turning to Bob he said,—

" Will you break the news to Widow Green, or must I?"

"You go, Cap'n, please," then answered Ned, appealingly.

The brave fellow who but a little while before had responded readily to the call on his strength and heroism, shrank from carrying bad news to the lonely widow, and from witnessing her tears of grief for him who had been her only support.

When Captain Lobb, in answer to Ned's appeal, had said, "All right, Ned, I will go, for you have done noble work to-day," the men dispersed, and went to their several homes; feeling sure that no one could tell the sad news so gently as their Captain.

In less than two hours the news had been told in every house in Treggonoweth. People spoke to each other in sadder, lower tones, and many a tear started to their eyes as they talked of the poor stricken mother. Many little gifts were sent by the kind-hearted, hard-working woman who had volunteered to spend the night at the widow's lonely house by the wayside. Wives were kinder to their husbands that evening, and many an almost forgotten luxury was cooked for "Tom" or "Jack's" supper. Husbands forgot to snarl at their wives or frown on their children, and sat by the fire with subdued looks on their faces.

Jacky Williams heard his father tell the news with mixed feelings of anger and consternation, and creeping away to bed where he could think undisturbed, he turned over the intelligence in his mind.

"Nicholas Green is dead," he reiterated to himself, "is dead and out of my reach. My plans are all useless; all that I have found out about him is of no use now, for what is the use in exposing a dead man? It would be cowardly to accuse a man who is not alive to defend himself. Neither my father or Bob will ever know how cleverly I found out their mystery. I hated Nicky Green when he was living, and I hate him more than ever now he is dead."

Poor sinful Jacky! He had allowed his evil passions to grow unchecked, and now they were almost beyond his control. His good qualities, for he had many were lulled to sleep; and a few more years of scheming and revenge, would make them sleep the sleep of death.

As he lay on his bed nursing his hatred, and thinking nothing of the terror which must have entered the heart of that poor sinful man, when the waters came rushing in about him, when all escape was cut off, and he was called on to face the king of terrors alone—he little thought what agony and remorse was in store for him.

Let us not judge him too hardly, for he had never seen death, nor ever followed a dear friend to the grave. He had seen many funerals, and had often made sarcastic remarks about those who gave vent to their grief in loud wails and cries, but personally he knew not what real grief was.

Jacky could not sleep that evening, and he was not sorry when his mother came to his bedside with a light. Sitting down and smoothing his golden hair with loving fingers she asked tenderly, "Isn't my Jacky well to night?"

" Rather tired, mother, that is all," said Jacky, the moisture starting to his eyes as he felt his mother's gentle touch.

" I thought you might be frightened at the news, for it is such a sudden thing. I've been wondering what his poor mother will do, for she has nobody to help her now that Nicky is dead," said Mrs. Williams pitifully. Jacky looked at his mother curiously, for she had reminded him that there was someone who loved Nicky Green, even as his mother loved him.

" I wonder if any one can be so bad but what a mother will love him," said Jacky, musingly.

" A true mother will love her son no matter what

he does, or how low he may fall," answered Mrs. Williams, thinking the question was addressed to her, " and a man isn't worthy the name of *man*, unless he respects his mother. I am not afraid but that my Jacky will always respect me."

" He will always love you, mother, as long as he lives, and that amounts to the same thing, doesn't it ? " asked Jacky, merrily.

" I don't think it does; for I think that love is something dearer than respect, though I reckon it is not so lasting. Men give their love to somebody else, but they've generally a little respect to bestow on their mother."

" You shall always have both from your son, mother dear; that will satisfy you, won't it ? " asked Jacky, patting his mother's hand caressingly.

" You are a good lad, Jacky, and mother doesn't believe anything against her boy. Father was worrying about something he had heard about you being at the " Golden Arms," and was going to talk to you about it, but I told him it was all nonsense, for my Jacky never kept anything from his mother, and was a good lad always, and nobody would make me believe otherwise. So I persuaded him out of the mind of bothering you about it, for what is the use of worrying before there's a cause ? "

"None in the world, mother, and you're a regular gem," answered Jacky, turning his crimson face away.

"There! I was sure it was all right. It is no use for your father to argue with me, is it, sonny?" asked Mrs. Williams, triumphantly.

"Not a bit, you're a regular philosopher, mother," answered Jacky laughingly, as his mother turned away.

"So father has been hearing things, has he?" thought Jacky.

"And mother has been arguing him out of believing them. Poor old darling, it is well for me that she has that weak point, though she considers it her strongest. People seldom see their weak points: so much the better for me."

And then Jacky fell to wondering how much his father knew. Somehow as he looked at his actions in the light in which his father would view them, they seemed despicable and small, and were robbed of all their smartness. He could not see that anything he had ever done, would raise him in his father's estimation, nay, he felt sure that he should sink very low if his father learnt all. Pride and vanity forsook him, and Jacky was thoroughly miserable and out of conceit with himself. That feeling was destined to be increased a hundred-fold.

E

As he sat by the table reading aloud to his mother the next evening—Hattie had gone to chapel and his father was in bed—Ned Trethewey's mother, who lived in the next house, came in with a scared look on her face and said, hurriedly:

"Have you heard this terrible news about Kitty Turner?"

"No. What is it?" asked Mrs. Williams quickly.

"Why she has been missing since yesterday, and no one knows where she is. Her father was up all last night searching for her, and all the day, but he cannot find a single trace of her."

"But where can she have gone? Where was she yesterday?" asked Mrs. Williams in consternation.

"She was at the Great Louisa Mine as usual, and was seen at her work, just before leaving work-time; but no one has seen her since. Her father is nearly crazy, for she was his darling, and her mother is fairly breaking her heart. I never heard anything so sad in my life," and Mrs. Trethewey wiped away a sympathetic tear from her eye.

"But there must be some reason for her leaving home so suddenly, for Kit Turner was too sensible a girl to leave a good home for nothing. And she was not the girl to destroy herself," then argued Mrs. Williams, practically.

"I don't know that," said Mrs. Trethewey in a mysterious whisper. "It is told all about that she and Nicky Green were courting, and some people think that when she heard he was drowned, that she went away and destroyed herself."

"Then if she has done that, she must have gone out of her mind, for Kitty Turner was too much afraid of death to do that in her right senses. It is my impression that there is something behind all this which we don't know, but it may come to the light." Then turning round as Mrs. Trethewey left the house, and catching sight of Jacky's face she exclaimed:

"Why, Jacky, my darling! what is the matter?"

CHAPTER VII.

REMORSE.

FEEL faint, I will go to bed," gasped Jacky, trying to collect his scattered thoughts, and turn his staring eyes from his mother's face.

"Dear, what a shock you gave me!" said Mrs. Williams, in breathless tones. "I thought you had a fit. Shall mother carry you to bed, you look so weak?"

"Yes, carry me, mother," whispered Jacky, with a sob. All his pride and dignity had fled, and Mrs. Williams held in her arms a little remorseful, weeping boy.

"There, my darling, mother will get you a nice cup of tea, and then you will soon be better. So much awful news has upset you, I expect. And no wonder, for I'm all in a tremble myself," and with tears in her kind eyes, Mrs. Williams went downstairs to make the tea which was to cure her boy.

There was no medicine for general purposes that Mrs. Williams had so much faith in as tea. If anyone had a headache, nothing was so sure to cure it as a cup of good strong tea. If you were sick, nothing would settle your stomach so quickly as tea; if you were tired, it would refresh you; sleepy, it would waken you. If you were heated, it would cool you; cold, it would warm you; cast down by grief, nothing so sure to brighten you as tea—in fact, like a good many other all-powerful medicines, Mrs. Williams recommended her favourite beverage as a cure for every ill that the flesh is heir to. She did not, however, consider that *one dose* would be sufficient, but recommended it both summer and winter, and all the year round.

Left to himself, Jacky wept tears of real grief, for he had always liked Kitty Turner; and it seemed terrible to him that she with whom he had talked only the day before should now be an inanimate corpse. Where was she lying? Had she thrown herself over a precipice, or had she drowned herself? "What! not that—no, not that!" gasped Jacky, starting up in bed as a horrible thought crossed his mind; and then he fell back stiff and motionless on his pillow.

When consciousness again returned, he lay with white, pain-drawn face, and fixed, staring eyes, like one insensible. In great alarm, Mrs. Williams would have sent for a doctor, but Jacky only begged to be allowed to sleep. He wanted to be alone, he told his mother, and she, good soul, accustomed to yield to his will, did so, after seeing him drink his tea, thinking that he would no doubt be all right by morning.

Poor little Jacky! All thoughts of revenge had fled, and remorse, strong and fierce, was tugging at his heart. Fearful visions were floating before his eyes, and crouching down in bed, he whispered in terror,—

"You would never have gone there but for me, Kitty. I am your murderer—I drove you to it! I did not care about Nicky Green being drowned; but you, Kit—you who would have been innocent but for him—that you should have been driven to your death by me, is more than I can bear, and live."

A blessed faintness again stole over him, and the visions melted away. After that, he fell into a kind of stupor, which lasted until morning. Weak, but with his mind restored to its wonted vigour, Jacky awoke with a heart weighèd down with such a load of misery as he had never thought it possible for one heart to carry. His mind was clearer than it had been the night before, and he was able to weigh the story he had heard carefully. Taking that story as it stood, it was quite possible that Kit Turner was alive, and might even be at home now, giving good reasons for her absence. Jacky tried to believe this, but could not. No reasoning would stand before the words he had heard her speak, " I will see him before I leave the mine."

Only *he* knew where to look for Kit Turner. Should he go to the grief-stricken father, and say :— " It is not anywhere on the surface that you must look for your daughter, nor is it of any use for you to drag the river; but wait until the engine at the Great Louisa Mine has done its work, then where they find Nicky Green you may expect to find your daughter ? "

Should he tell him this? and then, in answer to the questions which would be asked as to how he got his knowledge, should he add to the old man's too heavy load of grief by telling him why his daughter had sought Nicky Green, and in so doing had found her own death ? No ! a thousand times, No. Better let the old man search for her on the surface, with the faint hope of finding her, than to know that his daughter was lying drowned by the side of the man who had tempted her to be dishonest; and if the rushing water should carry her to some other part of the mine from where they found Nicky Green, no one would think of searching for her there, and the secret would be safe. It would be a relief to tell someone, a relief so great that no one—who did not, like Jacky, hold a fearful secret—could realise. But it was the only thing he could do for her, and cost him what it would, Jacky resolved that it should be kept.

Unable to go to school, and glad to escape from his mother's pitying glances, Jacky dragged his weary limbs out of the house. He did not mean to go to the mine, but something impelled him to do so. When he arrived there, he found the men standing around in groups. All underground work was suspended, and very little was done by any at the mine that day. The engine was being worked up to its full power, and Jacky shuddered as he thought that each powerful stroke was bringing the truth nearer to light.

A stranger, passing through the mine, would have seen at a glance that something was amiss. The men all spoke in hushed tones, and all eyes seemed to be directed towards the engine beam, which never before had been worked with such speed. Up and down it went with ominous velocity, and each time it went down with a plunge into the water, it forced up food for the unceasing stream, which was being carried off in another direction.

As Jacky listened to the admiring remarks which the men were making about the new engine, and heard their words of praise about her great power and speed, he forgot for a minute his misery. And as he looked at the "bob" going up and down without any cessation, he began to wish that it would stop a few minutes to rest, and he felt as if it must be tired; then, remembering that it was not a thing of life as the men's remarks would almost imply, he turned with a shudder to go away, when he heard a stranger say to one of the men,—

"How long do you expect it will be, before you will be able to search for your comrade?"

"If the engine is kept on all day and to-night at its present speed, we calculate to go down to-morrow forenoon," was the answer.

"And where do you expect to find him?"

"Just under the spot where that little lad is standing," answered the man, pointing to Jacky.

Jacky sprang aside as if the ground were red-hot; and leaving the mine, he went home as fast as his trembling limbs would carry him. Tottering into the house, and almost falling into his father's elbow-chair, the cold moisture broke out over his face and hands, and, rolling his eyes about in agony, he asked himself if the secret was ever to haunt him thus.

What fate had led him to stand on the very spot where Nicholas Green was supposed to be lying, and where Kitty Turner might also be for aught he knew? Should he be able to keep the secret and live, or would death soon put an end to his misery? Would death be the end of misery, or was it only the beginning, and that which he was suffering now only a faint foretaste? If death were an eternal sleep, how gladly would he die. His mother had said that he deserved heaven because of the affliction he had to bear; but affliction of the body was nothing to be compared to anguish of the mind. He knew that he had brought the latter on himself to get revenge; and as he reviewed the past with mind cleared of all sophistry, he plainly saw that he had brought the former on himself as well, by his wilfulness in disobeying his father.

He saw that his life had been a series of wrongdoings. Petty things some of them were, but always to resent some slight which someone had visited on him. Instead of ignoring those slights, and trying so to live as to win people's respect, he had sought to revenge himself by possessing their secrets, and threatening to disclose them.

Jacky saw now how ignoble were his aims, and how low was his ambition, and now he was reaping his reward. It was true, in Nicky Green's case he had only done what a great many others were doing —finding out and exposing theft and trickery; and had his motive been any other but revenge, he should not now be suffering such remorse. But when he remembered that it was to gratify his own petty pride that he had ferreted out the secret, and frightened Kitty Turner into seeking her own death, he could find no excuse for himself. Of Nicky Green he thought nothing, for he was underground by his own choice; but Kit Turner, that poor, ill-advised girl, would never have been there but for him.

Thus Jacky went on thinking all that weary day, eating scarcely anything, and speaking but little to anyone. As night came on, and darkness settled on the earth, Jacky began to wonder if he should sleep. He did not feel like it, for his brain seemed unnaturally active. He dreaded the visions which a sleepless night would conjure up before his eyes, and, starting up in desperation, he vowed that he would purchase sleep at any cost.

Once more he made use of his friend Sol, and that night, for the first time in his life, Jacky Williams was *drunk.*

CHAPTER VIII.

WHERE WAS SHE?

ACKY had vowed that he would purchase sleep at any cost, and he had done so; but it cost him one of the fearfullest headaches that ever racked a human head. And when he woke the next morning, and knew that he should have to suffer it all day, he acknowledged that he had only added to his misery, and to the many mistakes he had already made in his lifetime.

" I have got hold of the wrong end of life somehow," thought Jacky, remorsefully. " Everything I do seems to make me more miserable."

He felt too ill to leave his bed, but knowing that he could not rest there, he got out, although he was shaking like a man with the palsy. After drinking two or three cups of tea, and paying no heed to his mother's remonstrances, Jacky again started off for the mine. He dreaded going there, but until he knew whether Kit Turner's body was brought to the surface with Nicky Green's, he could not rest.

When he got to the mine he saw that the engine had slackened its speed, and that a crowd of men

was gathered around the shaft. As he drew near
he heard the whisper: "They are coming!" and a
minute later the dead body of Nicholas Green was
taken out of the "skip" and laid on a rude stretcher,
which was silently taken up by the men and carried
to the carpenter's shop.

With a great sigh of relief Jacky turned away.
Kit Turner was not found. But where was she?
Should he ever rest until he knew? Did she go
underground that day? She could not have gone
by the main footway without running the risk of
being seen by the men, and she would try to avoid
that if she could. Had she gone at all? and if so,
which way?

Walking out of the mine by another road to avoid
the people who were crowding around the carpenter's shop, Jacky sat down by the side of the hill to
think. The Great Louisa Mine stood on an emi-
nence, and on one side, where Jacky was sitting, it
gradually sloped down into a valley. From this
valley a tunnel had been driven, which intersected
the shaft at a depth of about twenty fathoms. It
was never used as a footway, it being more con-
venient for the miners to descend from the top of
the shaft, the entrance of the tunnel being so far
from their homes. Jacky knew of the existence of

this tunnel, and suddenly it occurred to him that if Kit Turner had gone underground at all, she had gone that way. What a fool he had been not to have thought of it before. He might have saved her life perhaps. Was it possible that she could be alive now?

She had been two days and two nights lost. He had heard of men being underground longer than that, and had been found alive. But Kitty was a woman, and though like other mine girls she had gone underground to see what it was. like many times, she was not inured to the darkness like men who habitually worked there. Still there was room for hope, and jumping up utterly forgetful of his weakness, Jacky dashed back to the smith's shop for candles. And then thinking that if she were living he should want something to help to restore her, he ran home with swift footsteps. Going to the cupboard he caught up an empty bottle and some biscuits; then rushing into the sitting-room he took his sister's smelling salts, and was out of the house again before his mother could get downstairs. Filling the bottle with water from the spring, Jacky ran with all his wonted swiftness back to the mine. Excitement gave him strength, and it was not long before he was again at the bottom of the hill, and lighting his candle, he walked with a beating heart into the level.

He had not walked more than half-a-mile before he saw her whom he was searching for. She was lying apparently lifeless on the ground, with a great cut on her forehead. Jacky shuddered as he looked at the deathly face, and then turned away from the fearful sight with a cry of fear. Repressing the inclination to run with a mighty effort, Jacky dropped on his knees, feeling that he wanted help, and knowing that there was only One who would come to his aid. In his excitement he forgot the candle he held, and it slipped from his grasp, but instead of being extinguished, it fell on its end into some mud and stuck there as securely as if it were in a candlestick.

"Thank the Lord," burst from Jacky as he saw it, for he felt if he were left in darkness with that fearful object behind him he should go mad. Clasping his hands over his face, he prayed as he had never prayed before in his life. He supplicated with terrible earnestness for restoration of life to the lifeless form behind him, promising that if such were granted, his own life should henceforth be dedicated to Him. He prayed that the murderer's stain might not rest on him, and that his soul might not be weighed down for all time with such a load of guilt as now oppressed him. In his agony he cried, " Lord, save *her* or I perish.

Jacky prayed earnestly and sincerely, and his prayer was answered, as all such prayers are. When he rose from his knees, there was peace in his soul, such as it had been an entire stranger to. Conquering his fear, Jacky turned and knelt down by the prostrate figure, and taking one hand in his, he rubbed it between his own. It was deathly cold, but limp, and remembering that he read somewhere the words, " his body stiffened in death," he took courage, and moistened the white lips with water, and put his sister's smelling salts to her nose.

For half an hour Jacky worked on patiently, and then he saw a flutter of one eyelid, and a twitching round the mouth. Dipping his handkerchief in a pool of water which was near, he bathed the cut on her head, and then tied the wet handkerchief on tightly. Seeing fresh signs of recovery after this, Jacky raised the poor girl to a sitting posture, and got some water down her throat. Soon he was rewarded by seeing the big blue eyes unclose, but they soon closed again. After pouring a few more drops of water down her throat, he soaked a little of the biscuit and put it in her mouth, which she swallowed much to Jacky's delight. When she opened her eyes again they seemed to be asking for more, and breaking the biscuit into small pieces he fed her slowly, for as soon as she began to eat, she ate like one starved. When she had eaten all the biscuits and drank the water, Jacky said, " Do you know me, Kitty?"

The girl looked at him steadily, but did not speak. Then suddenly clasping her hand to her bandaged head, she seemed to be puzzled, and asked in a whisper, " What have you done to my head?"

" You knocked it, I expect; but it will be better soon. Will you stand up now?"

" No, I'm tired," she answered, in the same voiceless whisper. " Let me lie down."

Seeing her head droop to one side, Jacky put her gently down, and hastily pulling off his jacket, he made it into a pillow for her head. Her eyes were closed, and he saw that she was asleep, for her breathing was regular, and again falling on his knees, Jacky thanked the Lord with a fervent heart for answering his prayer. Then rising and casting another look at the prostrate girl, he lit a second candle and walked quickly out of the level.

As soon as he emerged into the daylight, he started off to fetch Kitty's father, running at the top

F

of his speed. In the lane where he had once followed Kitty he saw her father walking along with feeble steps and bent head. Jacky hardly knew him at first, for those two days had made a brisk, hearty man of fifty look like an old man of eighty, and had bleached the iron-grey hair and whiskers to a snowy whiteness. Jacky laid his hand on the man's arm to attract his attention, and said, softly,—

"I have come to bring you tidings of Kitty."

The bent form straightened, hope lighted up the faded eyes, and grasping Jacky's arm, he asked, eagerly,—

"Where is she? Take me to her."

"Come with me and you shall see her," answered Jacky, turning and walking back with swift steps.

Scarcely a word was spoken until they reached the level, and then Jacky said,—

"She is in here. You must not be frightened, for she looks very ill," and without more words he lit his candle and led the way into the level.

They saw the light, but what was Jacky's horror and astonishment to find that the girl was gone.

"What is it?" asked Turner, as he heard Jacky's cry of fear.

"She is gone," gasped Jacky.

"What!" shouted the disappointed father. "You

have been deceiving me, you horrible little rascal,"
and taking Jacky by the collar, in a terrible rage, he
shook him until the poor lad gasped for breath, then
pushing him away with the last remnants of his
anger, he threw himself face downwards on the
ground, while great hoarse sobs of disappointment
shook his frame. When the sobs had died away,
Jacky said, in a choked voice,—

" If you will look around you, Mr. Turner, you will
see that I have not been fooling you. Here is the
candle which I dropped when I first caught sight of
her, and there by your side is my jacket which I put
under her head for a pillow, and here is the bottle
out of which she drank."

The father saw those things at a glance, and then
said, in grief-stricken tones, " Where can she be ?
And why was she here ?"

Jacky hesitated, fearing to increase the father's
misery. He saw this, and looking at Jacky sternly,
he said,—

" I asked why she was here, and how did you
know where to find her ?   Out with it, I say; tell me
every bit of the truth, or I'll shake the very life
out of your body."

Seeing that the man's usually quiet nature was
stirred to its depths, and fearing to further provoke

his wrath by withholding anything, Jacky told him all, sparing himself not in the least. He saw how the recital of the tale pierced the father's heart, soften it down as much as he would, and when the tale was finished, he said, in a broken voice,—

"Boy, I have wronged you, and I ask you to forgive a broken-hearted father."

"It is *I* that should ask forgiveness," said Jacky, in anguish. "I who drove your daughter here to gratify my own wicked vanity."

"You take too much blame to yourself, boy. My girl sinned, and she has been punished for her sin. But the man who led her into crooked ways—well, he is dead, let him rest. But enough; my girl is living somewhere; let us search."

Snatching the candle from Jacky, he held it down, and saw foot-prints which he knew were hers pointing towards the mouth of the level.

"She is gone out. Come along, boy," he cried, hastily.

Jacky caught up his jacket and followed.

CHAPTER IX.

HATTIE'S AWAKENING.

RACING the footprints, they saw that she had taken the straight road home. They had missed her by coming across fields by a nearer cut. Not far from her home they overtook her reeling along like a drunken woman. Fever had followed on unconsciousness, and had given her a fictitious strength. Throwing his arm around her, the father said in an unsteady voice,—

"Run on and tell mother that Kitty is found, and that she must get a bed ready. Tell her she is ill, and all depends on keeping her quiet. Thank God, mother can control herself in excitement."

Jacky ran on, and into the house. As he told his news and saw the mother's blanched cheeks and shaking hands, yet never heard a cry, and saw how quickly she set about her work, he felt that she justified her husband's praise.

It was well that Mrs. Turner could exercise self-control, for she had great need of it in the weary days of watching and nursing that followed.

Several weeks had passed before Kitty Turner's

brain was clear enough to allow her to give an explanation of her absence. By her own account, she had risked Nicky Green's displeasure by intercepting him on his way to the shaft, but that she had barely time to say " Jacky Williams knows all, and has left a message for you," when someone was seen approaching, and Nicky had answered, hurriedly, " Meet me at the old level down in the valley as soon as you leave work," and had then left her. So fearful of being seen talking to the girl he had led into sin did a guilty conscience make him.

Kitty never dreamed of disobeying Nicky, and so went to the "old level" as he had commanded. She waited for some time at the entrance, and then, fearing that her candle would not hold out, she walked on for some distance, expecting to meet Nicky at every step. *But he did not come.* She noticed as she was passing that one piece of wood overhead was dangerously low, it being almost broken in two, and she had to bend her head very low to pass without knocking herself. Getting uneasy at last, she stopped to listen, but she could hear nothing but a far-off rushing sound which filled her heart with terror, and turning, she ran wildly towards the entrance, quite forgetful of the piece of shelving wood. She knew not how long she lay on the ground unconscious, but when she came to herself she was in pitchy darkness, and with only a dim recollection of where she was. She had an impression that she must get out, but which was the way *out* or *in* she knew not. She walked on and on in a confused way, for what seemed an endless distance, but no glimmer of light greeted her tired eyes; and then she turned and walked back again.

" I fancy I must have struck myself a second time against that piece of wood, for I don't remember anything more until I found myself here," said Kitty, as she told the story to her mother. " You know all about it now, mother, and why I went there, and I am glad, for it has taken a load off my mind, though at one time I thought I would rather die than let you and father know what a sinner I had been. You have both forgiven me, and now I want you to forgive Nicky. He is wicked, I know, but he is not all bad. And, oh, mother, can't you see I love him, and always shall. You will, won't you, for my sake, mother? and then I can send for him to come to see me!" and the poor girl turned her white, worn face towards Mrs. Turner with such an earnest, pleading look on it, that, knowing what she knew, it was almost too much even for her self-control.

Kitty knew nothing of what had happened, for not until all risk of a relapse had passed would they tell her what would almost break her faithful heart. Stifling her emotion, Mrs. Turner answered—

"Yes, dear, father and I have both forgiven him."

"Thank you, mother, so many times," and Kitty threw her wasted arms around her mother's neck and gave her a grateful kiss, and then said, softly, "I am so happy. I seem to have nothing left to wish for."

Poor Kit Turner! It was the last time she was ever heard to say that she was happy.

But we have been running ahead with our story, and must now return to Jacky, who, when he had seen Kitty taken upstairs, and knew that he could be of no further use, left the house.

Now that the excitement was over, overtaxed nature gave way, and he had not walked very far before he fell helpless by the side of the road. Consciousness did not forsake him, but he felt too weak to move.

"I will lie here and rest a little while," he thought.

Spite of the weakness which seemed to be overpowering him, Jacky felt happier than he had been for many a long day. He had done something now for which his conscience gave him approval. For the last two days he had been living through a time of terrible excitement and remorse, and the feeling of peace which he now felt, arising from repentance for sin and the forgiveness of God, was altogether so new and delightful that he forgot everything else as he lay there. Soon the delicious feeling of peace gradually deepened into sleep, and he slept undisturbed by a single dream.

He was awakened by a voice saying—

"Why, Jacky, what are you doing here? You will catch your death of cold, lying on this wet grass."

Looking up, he saw Bob Trethewey's honest eyes gazing down at him.

"Is that you, Bob?" he asked, feebly.

"Yes, but what's the matter, little chap?" asked Bob, stooping and lifting him in his strong arms. Jacky clasped his arms around Bob's neck, and laying his cheek against the other's, he said, with a soft sigh of satisfaction,—

"Dear old Bob, you'll carry me home, won't you?"

"Certainly, my boy. It's not the first time you've had a ride in my arms. I remember carrying your sister, too; it was when the roads were so slippery her little feet could not carry her."

If Jacky had not been so sleepy he might have felt the cheek next his grow hot.

"She was a little girl then, very different from what she is now, so dreamy and quiet," continued Bob, softly. "She was not so shy with me then, but it's not much wonder, for there's nothing for such as her to see in a rough chap like me." And then Bob walked on in silence, forgetting almost that Jacky was in his arms.

When they came to the gate, Bob said, with a shy laugh,—

"I'd better carry you in, I reckon, little man, just like I used to."

Jacky roused up at that, and said, "Yes, please, Bob." And then smiling a little, he whispered, slyly, with something of his old mood, "Hattie will be home by this time. You'll like seeing her, aye, old man?"

Bob laughed and reddened still more, then entering the house after a little preliminary knock, he said, laughingly, "Here's your truant son, Mrs. Williams. He was so tired or lazy, that like the pig that went into the woods to grow fat, he has had to be carried home."

Bob was placing him gently on a chair, but Jacky held on and said,—

"Carry me up to bed, Bob. I'm too tired for anything else."

As Bob looked at Jacky's now crimson cheeks and glittering eyes, and felt the burning hands on his neck, he said to Mrs. Williams, significantly:

"He is right, ma'm, that is the best place for him." And then carrying him upstairs he undressed him, and laid him in bed, tucking the clothes around him with a touch as gentle as a woman's.

" Good-night, dear old Bob. Don't let the candle drop into the mud like I did. She wasn't there, was she, Bob?"

"She! who?" asked Bob, looking at Jacky anxiously.

" What did I say? Oh, my head is so bad. Do you think I am going to be ill?" and Jacky looked piteously into Bob's face.

" I hope not. You must keep still and go to sleep if you can."

" I will try; but my head roars so. It was the noise of the water, I expect, that made her head split. Take me home, Bob, I'm so tired. Good-night," and the lids dropped over the bright eyes, and Jacky slept.

With a seriously alarmed face, Bob went downstairs, and said to Mrs. Williams, " Do you know what is the matter with him? Has he been ill?"

Mrs. Williams told how he had been, and then

starting up, she said, anxiously, "You don't think he is very ill, do you?"

"I am afraid he is," answered Bob, gravely. "He seems to be all wrong in the head."

"Why; he seemed all right with you just now, I thought," said John Williams, with a disturbed look on his face, and then jumping up, forgetful of his lame foot, he said, hurriedly, "I'll go at once for the doctor."

"No; sit down, man, you can't go. I'll borrow a horse and be there and back again before you could get half-way. Don't be alarmed, it may be only a feverish cold. I'll call in again when I come back, so I won't say good-night," and Bob cast a look at Hattie as he moved towards the door. But Hattie took no notice of him, for she was gazing into the fire with a disturbed look on her face.

"She is not without a heart, if she is cold. Perhaps if Jacky is ill it will wake her up a bit," and shutting the door softly after him, Bob hastened away.

Jacky slept on until the doctor came. Obediently he held out his arm and put out his tongue, and then looking at the doctor with a smile, he said,—

"I don't think there is much the matter with me, except my head?"

"That's right, little man. Always keep a brave heart."

As the doctor was examining him, and felt the large hump on his back, an exclamation of pity burst from his lips. This seemed to excite Jacky, and pulling up the clothes around him, he said, angrily,—

"I don't want your pity; keep it." Then his mood changed, and stretching out his hands very imploringly, he said, "Don't stay here, doctor; go to her. I tied up her head, but it wasn't done properly. Her head was split in two; I wish mine was. Can't you open it and let the pain out," and Jacky rolled his head from side to side, and moaned like one in great pain.

"His mind is wandering a little," said the doctor as he left the room. "I will tell the young fellow who is waiting for the medicine to bring back some ice to put on his head, for he has all the symptoms of brain fever. In the meantime bathe his head with vinegar, and keep him as quiet as possible. Humour him in everything, and don't let him get excited."

Late that evening Hattie came softly to her mother's side, as she sat by Jacky, and said in a whisper,—

"You go and lie down, mother, and let me stay with Jacky for an hour or two."

"You! why what good would you be here? You would forget when to give him his medicine, and everything else, for you know how absent-minded you are. No, no, go away to bed. You can't do anything here, and I don't want to have you ill, too."

Mrs. Williams had no thought of being unkind, and Hattie knew it, but all the same she went away with a heavy heart. Going down-stairs again, she sat with her face buried in her hands, while she tried to choke down the sobs that were rising in her throat. She was deeply disappointed, not only at being kept from her brother, but with herself. Never before had she seen how useless she was in the home circle.

In all the old bygone tales she had read women had played brave parts. They had cheered their husbands and lovers when they were going to the wars, bound up their wounds and nursed them when they came back. While some had followed their loved ones to the field of battle, and had in many instances saved their lives, and when not able to do that they had stayed by them and soothed them in their dying hours. Florence Nightingale and Grace Darling, though working in different ways, had both worked nobly to save and to rescue their fellow creatures.

All her life Hattie had wanted to be a heroine, and

to do some noble deed. She had dreamed of herself as taking a part in all sorts of stirring adventures, but her dreams were over, the awakening had come, and it was a sad one.

Hattie had always thought that if women had one talent that was more to be admired than another, it was for nursing. In the hospital, on the field of battle, or in the private sick-room, her skill was acknowledged, and her presence was indispensable. But here, at the only opening which was left to her wherein she could follow the example of her illustrious and heroic sisters, she had been told that she was not fit for the work. Hattie loved her brother in her dreamy fashion, but she never thought of his being in any great danger, and she grieved more over her own inefficiency than she did at her brother's illness.

She was sitting gazing listlessly into the fire, when there came a gentle knock at the door, followed immediately by Bob Trethewey. Hattie looked up as Bob came in, and seeing the sorrowful look on her face, he felt a great desire to comfort her, and said, cheerily,—

" Don't look so sad, Hattie. I hope Jacky will be better in a few days. In the meantime you must give him real good nursing, for that is half of the work."

"But mother won't let me," said Hattie, with a sob. "She says I'm no good there, for I'm so absent-minded. I should forget his medicine and everything else," and she buried her face in her hands and wept bitterly.

"Poor child!" said Bob, soothingly. He wanted to comfort her, but hardly knew what to say, for he felt that Mrs. Williams was right. At last he said, "Never mind, if you can't nurse Jacky you can help your mother with the house-work, for she can't be upstairs and down too."

"Yes, but I never heard of Florence Nightingale doing house-work, but she nursed the sick," and Hattie looked up at Bob with tears still standing in her great dreamy eyes.

"Ah! I see," said Bob, nodding his head with a knowing smile. And then bending towards Hattie he said, earnestly, "But while Florence Nightingale was nursing the sick and wounded in a hospital, weren't the wives and mothers and sisters of those soldiers at home doing house-work? They had to take care of the children who called those men father, and keep the homes together, so that when the soldiers were pensioned off, or the war ended, they might have a home to come to. Most of those women had to work as well as pray, and when news came home that their loved ones would answer no more to the 'call to arms,' did they give up and spend their lives in tears? No, they worked on and brought up their children in the best manner they could. Such women as those are every-day heroines. They do not receive the praise of nations, and are unknown to the world in general; but, thank God, there is One above who knows them, and will reward them, too. Up there they will one day take rank with Florence Nightingale and a host of others whom this world delights to honour."

CHAPTER X.

On the Border Land.

ATTIE looked at Bob in surprise, for she had never heard him so eloquent before. She knew that he held some strange views about women, and he loved and respected his mother more than most young men. She knew also that his father was killed when Bob was but a small lad, and that Mrs. Trethewey had struggled on with her three children, receiving no help from anyone, until Bob was old enough to be taken on at the mine. She was well aware that Bob had had but little education, and she wondered how he should be able to talk so well. She had always thought of him, in her dreamy way, as a quiet, good-humoured, uninteresting young fellow; but here was an awakening on another point.

Starting to an upright position, and hurriedly taking some parcels from his pockets, Bob said, ruefully,—

"What a duffer I am to stay here talking and forget Jacky. You had better take this medicine up to your mother, and here is the ice and some grapes—they will be nice and cooling now that he is so feverish."

Hattie obeyed, and in a few minutes returned, and said, in a low voice,—

" Mother is *very* much obliged to you for your kindness and for being so thoughtful, for she thinks he will like the grapes; and she bids me tell you that Jacky is sleeping, and she hopes he will be better when he awakes."

" I am very glad to hear it," said Bob, heartily. " And now I must be going, and I would advise you to go to bed. If you bank up the fire, and put the kettle on, and turn down the lamp, I expect that will be all you can do for your mother, unless you should happen to rise early, and make her a nice cup of tea. Good night," and without casting a second glance at Hattie's crimson cheeks, Bob was gone.

The truth was, Hattie had never thought of doing those commonplace things which Bob had mentioned so quietly. He, a man, knew more what ought to be done in such an emergency than she did.

" What an ignorant, useless creature I am!" thought Hattie, remorsefully. " Why, Bob would be of more service to mother than I am,"

She did not know how many times Bob had been left when a lad to cook the meals and take care of his little sisters, while his mother was away earning bread for her children. And even when he was a young man, Bob had thought it no disgrace to help his tired mother with the housework.

With burning cheeks, Hattie did the things which Bob had mentioned; and then, with noiseless footsteps, betook herself to bed. She rose early the next morning; and after stirring the fire; and putting on fresh coals, she made the tea and got breakfast, and then stealing upstairs, she said, coaxingly,—

" There's a beautiful cup of tea downstairs, mother. I'll stay with Jacky while you are away, and it will be a change for him to have me here."

Seeing that Jacky's eyes were partly closed, and that he was almost asleep, Mrs. Williams consented to go down and get her breakfast.

" Do you know me, Jacky?" asked Hattie, gently, as she laid her soft hand on his forehead.

Jacky jerked his head away, and, looking at her with a wild light in his eyes, he asked, " Who are you?"

" I am Hattie, your sister, and I am going to stay here with you a little while, if you will let me. May I?"

Some recollection seemed to be stirred in Jacky's mind, for the tears sprang to his eyes, and, as he put up his little thin hand to wipe them away, he murmured, sadly,—

"She never thinks or cares about me. One of those fine people in her book is more to her than I am. She takes no more interest in me than if I were a dog—not so much, for she would pat a dog, but she never touches me." And then, sitting up in bed, he shouted, "Ah, ah! it'll take down your pride, Miss Hattie, when you hear that your brother is a murderer!"

"What! oh, what do you mean, Jacky?" asked Hattie, tremblingly.

Jacky took no notice of her; but, putting out his hands as if to ward off someone, he cried,—

"Go away, Kit! Why do you haunt me with your white, wet face? Go away! I can't bear it!"

He uttered those last words with a shriek, and then fell back exhausted on his pillow.

Mrs. Williams came hurrying into the room, and darting an angry look at Hattie, she pushed her aside, and laying her hand on Jacky's head, she said, soothingly,—

"What is it, darling? Mother is here now. It is all right; nothing can harm you."

The wild light died out of Jacky's eyes, and, clasping his mother's hand between his own, he said, trustfully,—

" You'll keep her away, won't you, mother? For you always loved Jacky, though he was only a poor little hunchback."

" Always, my darling; and nothing shall come near you while mother is here. Now, try to go to sleep again."

Hattie left the room and the house. Going to the schoolmaster, she told him that Jacky was ill, and asked him to excuse her from school for a day or two. The old man kindly consented, looking pityingly at her white face, but wondering at the look of horror in her no longer dreamy grey eyes. Hattie gave him no time to ask questions; but, walking back swiftly by the way she had come, she went home. Going to her bedroom, and locking the door behind her, she threw herself on the bed, and lay there like one stunned. She did not moan or cry, her grief was too deep for that. Her eyes had been partly opened by Bob's words the night before, and Jacky's wild speech had completed the work. She saw herself in her true colours for the first time in her life; and, in the light of Jacky's words, she felt that in dreaming of being a heroine she had been less than a woman. Girls whom she had looked on as common-place and not worthy of notice, were kinder, nobler, and more heroic than she. They in their daily lives were gentle and kind to their little brothers and sisters, and took an interest in all their doings, while she, with her high aspirations and exalted views, had, as her brother said, taken less notice of him than she would of a dog.

She had read of the sweet and holy influence which some sisters exerted over their brothers, and of their being the guardian angels in the home circle; but how far was she removed from those gentle loving girls. What kind of an influence had she exerted over her brother? She would have answered, "None at all," but the remembrance of Jacky's sad words made her stop and ask herself if her very indifference towards him had not been as an evil influence? That he cared about it she knew by his manner. To what depths had he fallen? and why did he call himself a murderer? He might be delirious, but something of truth was at the bottom. Vague rumours of the mischievous tricks he had played on the frequenters of the "Golden Arms," which she had taken no notice of at the time, came back to her now. Then there were his words about

Kit Turner, who was missing, and supposed to be dead. What had Jacky to do with her disappearance?

Horrible thoughts crowded in on Hattie's mind, until her head became giddy, and she felt sick and faint. When her mother called softly to her to go downstairs, she was so bewildered that she passed Mrs. Trethewey in the doorway without seeing her.

"I came to tell you that Kit Turner has been found. She is very ill, but the doctor thinks she will pull through, though he is afraid she will not be quite right in her head any more."

It was some time before Hattie could comprehend those words, but when she did, she burst into a flood of tears. They were blissful tears, though, and cleared her brain as nothing else would have done. Now that she knew Kit Turner was alive, Hattie felt that she could bear all the rest. She no longer felt hurt at not being allowed to nurse Jacky, for she humbly acknowledged that she had not the skill for such a delicate task. All that she could do to help her mother was done, and no housework was too mean for Hattie Williams to put her hands to after that day.

In the meantime, Jacky was in a raging fever. He was living those last two days over again in his mind, and talked incessantly of Kit Turner and Nicky Green. Sometimes he would be begging the engine to stop, and at others he would be praying that Kit Turner might live. When in the afternoon the sound of the bell tolling reached his ears, he clutched his mother's hand fearfully, and said:—

"Hark! do you hear the bell, mother? They have found Nicky Green, and he is going to be buried. There! they are lowering him into the grave, and now the parson is saying, 'Earth to earth, ashes to ashes.' Hear how the earth rattles down on the coffin! Hark, that is his mother! How she moans, just like the wind when it blows around the house before it comes to rain!" Then, clasping his hot hands together, he sang the following hymn:—

Thee we adore, eternal Name!
And humbly own to Thee!
How feeble is our mortal frame,
What dying worms we be!

These words, sung to a well-known funereal tune, in Jacky's sweet, boyish voice, was more than Mrs. Williams could bear; and, burying her face in her apron, she gave way to a fit of noiseless weeping. For a week the fever held its sway, and Mrs.

Williams never left her darling for more than a few minutes at a time. What sleep she had was when Jacky was sleeping, and she lay down by his side. The faintest moan would wake her, and day and night she tended and soothed him without a thought of her own weariness. Her very life seemed joined to his, and she had no thought for anything outside that sick room.

At the end of a week the fever left him, and Jacky lay with closed eyes and scarcely perceptible breath, only waiting, it seemed to those who watched by his side, for the good angel who should come to convey his soul into the spirit-world.

Suddenly he opened his eyes, and looked at his father and sister, and, seeing that they were both weeping, a smile of joy lit up his face, and he whispered,—

" I never thought you loved me so much; but don't cry, for I have never been of any use to any one."

Then he turned his eyes towards his mother, and, as he did so, a spasm of pain chased the smile away, and, as she stooped to wipe the cold sweat from his forehead, he whispered, " If you were only going with me, mother dear, I should die content."

" I shall not be long, my darling," answered Mrs.

Williams, with a smile on her white face. " Mother will not live long without her boy."

A look of sweet peace was imprinted on Jacky's face, and breathing a soft sigh, he rested his cheek on his hand, and slept.

CHAPTER XI.

A Sister Indeed.

HEN Jacky had got down so near to the Jordan that he could hear the surging of the waters on its banks, and when those who watched him thought that his soul had drifted out on the ocean, the tide of life slowly returned, and the watchers saw that he drew his breath with stronger respirations, while the deathly hue on his face gave place to a more life-like colour. This was the turning-point; and, as each wave of the incoming tide brings the water a little nearer to the shore, so each day brought back strength to Jacky's feeble frame. A fortnight later he was so much better that he was able to be taken out of bed. As he sat by the fire, wrapped in warm shawls, a smile played over his white face, and, nestling down among the cushions, he said,—

"This is delightful, Hattie. I hope mother is enjoying being out in the open air as much as I am being out of bed. I am glad she has gone out with father for a walk, it will do her good. It is nice weather for November, too, isn't it?'

" Yes, very. Quite an ideal Sabbath Day, so peace-
ful and so different from any other day," answered
Hattie, as she looked out of the window.

It was a rural scene on which her gaze rested, one
which she had seen many times before, but that day
it had taken on fresh beauties. The day was a quiet,
drowsy one. Not a leaf stirred, and no sounds but
the gentle twittering of birds or the crowing of a
cock at a distant farmyard could be heard. How
hushed and calm everything was, and how void of
bright colours everything looked. Soft, grey clouds
covered nearly all the sky, only a small opening now
and then showed there was blue underneath. Most
of the hills and fields were brown, as were the hedges,
and the moors were covered with patches of brown
ferns. A field here and there looked green, though
not the tender fresh green of spring. But all was
harmonious. Sky, and hills, and fields harmonised
with each other, and made up a pleasing picture
which was fair to look at.

Hattie's thoughts, neither merry or sad, seemed in
keeping with the scenery, and she was falling into
one of her old dreaming reveries, when Jacky roused
her by saying, musingly,—

" How strange life is, and what unforeseen things
happen ! A fortnight ago I never thought to have

left my bed again alive." Then he added, softly
and shyly, for, boylike, he felt diffident about speaking
out his higher thoughts, "God has been a great deal
kinder to me than I deserved."

"He is that to all of us," answered Hattie, in low
moved tones. "A fortnight ago I was afraid that
you would never know how sorry I am for my neglect
of you in the past. But in the future, God helping
me, you shall have a sister indeed as well as in
name."

"Do you really mean that, Hattie?" asked Jacky,
excitedly.

"Yes, Jacky, from the very bottom of my heart,"
and, kneeling in front of him, Hattie clasped her arms
around the little form, and pressed a loving kiss on
the white face. Placing his arms around his sister's
neck, and laying his cheek against her's, Jacky silently
expressed his joy in a way that was sweeter than
words. For some minutes they remained thus, and
then, remembering her mother's instructions, Hattie
unclasped her brother's arms from her neck, and
placing him again comfortably among his pillows, she
said, with a bright smile,—

"We shan't be able to persuade mother to go out
for a walk again if I do not take proper care of you.
I am going to get you something nice, and you must

eat every bit of it, or else I shall think I have done you harm by this talk."

"No you haven't, for happiness never hurts any-one, I'm sure," said Jacky, with a glad light in his eyes.

Much to Hattie's satisfaction Jacky did justice to the nice piece of fowl that she brought him, and, as she was taking the empty plate away, he said, laughingly,—

"There, I couldn't have done better if mother had been at home."

When she came into the room again the smile on Jacky's face had given place to a look of deep sad-ness.

"What is it that is troubling you?" asked Hattie, kindly.

"I have been wondering if it is possible to undo the past?" answered Jacky, looking wistfully at his sister.

"Do you mean as it stands toward God, or toward man?"

"Both; for I have sinned against God, and behaved badly towards a good many people."

"We cannot undo the past; for what has been done cannot be undone, but if we are truly repentant, and turn our back on ' the sin which doth so easily beset us,' we are sure of the forgiveness of God, and we know that He will blot out our sins, and 'remember them against us no more for ever.' As regards man, continued kindness will make most people forget past offences."

"I have made my peace with God, but not with man. How shall I go about it, Hattie?" asked Jacky.

"I don't think," said Hattie "we can lay down any hard and fast line, for opportunities for doing acts of kindness come in ways which we should never dream of. One thing I can point out to you in which you may do both men and their wives a great kindness, and that is as regards the 'Golden Arms.' I would not revive painful memories if I did not, think some good might come of it; but have you not by your music, enticed men to go to that place?"

"I am afraid I have, many times," answered Jacky, sorrowfully; "but it shall never be so again, and I will be a total abstainer for the rest of my life."

"Well done, Jacky. If you keep that resolve, you will increase your influence for good for the *rest of your life*. I was going to say that you know the old saying about landlords fiddling men inside their doors, and kicking them out; well instead of fiddling men into the public-house, I want *you* to fiddle them out," said Hattie, laughingly.

"Go on," said Jacky, the cloud that had settled on his face lifting a little at her bright words.

"You said just now that you were going to be a teetotaler. Now, suppose you make your violin a teetotaler also."

Falling in with her humorous vein Jacky laughed and said, "All right. It shall never be screwed *tight* any more. Go on, Hattie."

"When there is anything going on at the 'Golden Arms,' suppose you call in at the new temperance house which has been opened on the other side of the street, and take your teetotal violin with you. Mr. Warne is very fond of music. and is pretty sure to ask you to play, and if, as I suspect, your music has enticed men into a public-house, why may it not draw them into a temperance house, where are scattered around on the tables good readable literature, and where they might spend a cosy and profitable evening?"

"Whether the venture is successful or not, and I do not see why it might not be, it shall be tried if ever I get strong again. You have given me a motive in life, Hattie. While I have been lying on my bed thinking over my past sinful and useless life, I have almost wondered why God allowed me to be brought into the world, for there seemed nothing

H

that a poor little hunchback could do. But I don't think so now."

"Neither do I, for I believe that God has a purpose in life for every man and woman in the world, and if we see work before us and do not do it, woe be unto us. But if we cannot see anything to do, and do not care to search for it, then I believe that we shall have to give an account for the time we have wasted; for nothing but utter loss or lack of brain power can excuse either man or woman for not doing some kind of work in the world. There is work for all if we search for it, and I am truly glad that it is so, for I can conceive of no one more truly miserable than the person who has nothing to do."

"You never used to think like this, Hattie, did you?" asked Jacky wonderingly.

"No, dear, I was too much wrapped up in idle dreams to trouble my head about real work. I was always dreaming of doing, but never did anything. I should not be surprised if there were a good many in the world like me. Girls, I mean, for I think as a rule that men dream less than women, and they also trouble less about the future. They have more confidence in themselves, for they know that to a certain extent they must make their own future.

But women, or rather girls, expect to have their 'future' made for them, and so are always dreaming and wondering vaguely what it will be like."

"Girls are very strange, I think," said Jacky in his grave, old-fashioned way. "No matter how badly a fellow may act, if a girl really loves him, she will make excuses for him, and stick to him through thick and thin."

"Yes, I believe you are right," answered Hattie, smiling as she spoke. "I don't know whether the trait is most to be admired or deplored. I have read somewhere that women will stick to a sinking cause much longer than a man will."

"And I admire them all the more for it," said a manly voice outside. And then the door of the sitting-room was pushed open a little further, and Bob Trethewey's smiling face was inserted in the opening.

"Why, here's Bob," said Jacky in delighted tones. "Come right in, old fellow; don't you see that I'm downstairs?"

"Why, yes, and that will account for no one answering my knock at the door, and also for my over-hearing what you said just now," said Bob with a merry twinkle in his eyes. And then, turning to Hattie, he said comically: "I think this little man is rather young to have found out that girls are strange creatures, don't you ?"

" He has a sister, you see," said Hattie, demurely. Bob looked as if he did see the " sister," and with admiring eyes, too.

"But, Hattie, I didn't mean you!" said Jacky, eagerly. And then he added, correcting himself, " Perhaps you are a little bit strange; but then it's in a kind of nice way."

" That's just the way they all have, Jacky," said Bob, confidentially. " And that is one great reason why they have such influence over men. Doctor Parker says, ' If women would preach, surely the world would listen.' And, again, ' It is because woman can be so heavenly that she can be so low, and wicked and bad; it is because she can be so like a Saviour, that she can be such an engine and agent of ruin.' I believe that he is right, for I have known many a man whose life has been shipwrecked through a woman's treachery."

" And could not the same thing be said of the men ?" asked Hattie, with kindling eyes. " Are there not thousands of women to-day whose lives have been ruined by the treachery of men ? And as a rule it is the women who have to suffer most, for they must suffer in silence. Washington Irving

says, ' As the dove will clasp its wing to its side and
cover and conceal the arrow that is preying on its
vitals, so it is the nature of woman to hide from the
world the pangs of wounded affection.' I do not
deny that we wield a powerful influence over the
men, but they have as great, if not greater influence
over us, and there is no use their shifting all the re-
sponsibility on our shoulders, for we are all equally
responsible."

" You are right, Hattie, and that is the reason I
think why men and women should work *together*,"
said Bob, in low, significant tones.

Hattie did not answer, but rising hastily, she bent
over Jacky to re-arrange his shawls, for he had fallen
fast asleep. Though Hattie did not answer, Bob
was not displeased, nay, he felt better pleased than
if she had answered him. He didn't exactly know
why, unless it was that it showed something like a
lack of self-control on her part, and for once Bob
felt quite at ease, and master of himself in the com-
pany of this cold, dreamy, self-possessed girl. And
what was it that had caused Hattie to hide her face
from Bob's view, and kept it crimson long after he
had taken her hand in his and said " Good afternoon?" She did not know and could not explain it
even to herself, only after that, Bob occupied a much

larger share of her thoughts than he had hitherto done.

That evening, as Hattie stood by Jacky's bedside, and with unwonted fondness kissed his pale cheek, Jacky returned the caress, and then holding her face close to his, he said, huskily, " You have redeemed your promise already of being a true sister, Hattie, and in return I promise you that I will be a better brother, one that you shall not be ashamed of. And what little influence I may or shall possess, shall be used on the side of goodness and Temperance. And my teetotal violin shall never more be used to fiddle men into the " Golden Arms."

A few months later, when the warm weather had set in, Jacky and Hattie were sent to the sea-side. Jacky had not quite recovered his strength, while Hattie, who had been working hard over her examinations needed a change and rest. They had selected a quiet spot, which had not as yet become fashionable. They were seated one bright, breezy morning at the foot of a cliff which rose to a height of a hundred feet. The sea was calm, and the dark blue waters sparkling in the sunshine, looked innocent and safe, and seemed to invite one for a sail on its cool depths.

The brother and sister had been silent for some time, as they sat watching the waves rolling in

,

sometimes listening to the soft wash of the waves
on the pebbly beach, and at others listening to
the sea-gulls as they hovered overhead and uttered
their wild, plaintive cries.

"I wonder what they are saying to each other,"
said Jacky, at last, as he gazed up at those white,
beautiful birds. "May be they are singing, but if so,
their songs don't seem to be in tune with this calm
sea and sunny sky."

"Perhaps they are like the sailors, for I have heard
that on calm sunny days they sit around on deck
smoking and mending their clothes and telling of
terrible storms and shipwrecks, and of hair-breadth
escapes; and those beautiful birds what might they
not tell? What sights they must witness as they
fly over sea and land. I always fancy that weird
monotonous chanting of their's means something if
we could only interpret it."

A few minutes later Jacky said, "Will you give
me mother's letter, Hattie? I should like to read
again what she says about Kit Turner."

Hattie passed him the letter, and Jacky turned to
the paragraph in which his mother wrote: "Kit
Turner came to see me yesterday. She called to know
how Jacky was. A smile, the first I have seen on her
face since she was ill, lit up her face when I told her how

much better you were. She says she is getting quite strong again, but she does not look so. Her face is so white and thin, and there is always such a sad look in her eyes, just as if she were looking at Nicky Green's grave. Her mind is quite right now, and I think there is no longer any need to fear that the horror she must have suffered while underground, and the shock she received when told of Nicky's death, will bring on softening of the brain."

As Jacky folded the letter and passed it back to Hattie, he said, with a look of happiness beaming on his face, " Mother's letter was all that was wanting to complete my happiness, for she has taken away my last care. Isn't it jolly to think that father and mother are coming here to spend a week before we go home. Father and Bob must surely be making a fortune out of that piece of ground. I wonder if Bob will come with them ? I hope he will, he's such a good fellow."

Hattie did not answer, but looked quietly out at sea.

" Somehow, I fancy he will, for he is mixed up so in our affairs that he seems like one of the family,'' continued Jacky. And then, with one of his old-time chuckles, he said, " I rather think that Bob would like to have me for a brother, Hattie ?"

Still no answer from Hattie, though her mouth twitched, and her eyes brimmed over with laughter. As he looked at his sister, Jacky became serious in a moment, and said, in hurt tones,—

"I don't think there is any reason for you to laugh at Bob, Hattie. He is not handsome, I know, but he is one of the best men living; and I don't believe that there is a nobler, kinder heart in all the wide world than beats in Bob Trethewey's bosom. *You* may not think much of him, for I suppose he will not compare, in your estimation, with the spindle-shanked, kid-gloved dandies who figure as heroes in your books; but he is my friend, and for my sake I hope you will be kind enough not to laugh at him."

Hattie turned her now serious face towards Jacky, and said, softly,—

"You are right, Jacky, as regards Bob, but a little mistaken as regards your sister; for the day has passed when she thought that heroes were only to be found on the battle-field. My views have changed, and the man who does his duty bravely in spite of adverse circumstances, and who puts his own life in danger that he may save another, and withal is modest and *good*, is in my eyes a hero of the right kind."

"Yes, that is very good as regards men in general, but what about Bob in particular?" asked Jacky, half quizzically, half in earnest.

"We will not particularise, if you please; but if you aren't satisfied, ask Bob when he comes."

Whether Jacky ever did this or not we cannot say; but a week later, when he saw Bob helping Hattie into a boat, his mother heard him laugh in his own peculiar way, and say, as he rubbed his hands softly together, "Well done, little Jacky."

A. CROMBIE'S
New ✤ and ✤ Recent ✤ Books.

SILAS K. HOCKING'S POPULAR WORKS.

300,000 copies of this Author's books have been sold.

UP THE RHINE AND OVER THE ALPS.

BY S. K. HOCKING, F.R.H.S., author of "Her Benny," "His Father,"
"Dick's Fairy," "Sea Waif," &c., &c.   *With numerous Illustrations.*
Crown 8vo, cloth gilt, and gilt edges, 2*s.* 6*d.*

In crown 8vo, cloth gilt, gilt edges, 2s. 6d.

CALEB CARTHEW:

A Life Story.

With Steel Portrait.

"'Caleb Carthew' is no ordinary book, and the best may yet learn much that is good from its perusal. A very earnest, manly tone runs through 'Caleb Carthew.'"—*Morning Post.*

"Is full of sustained interest to the end."—*Literary World.*

"The story is, in fact, very much on the model of 'John Halifax, Gentleman,' though it is not in the smallest degree an imitation of that book. It is vigorously and pathetically told, and will enhance the author's reputation."—*Scotsman.*

In royal 16mo, cloth gilt, 1s.

OUR JOE.

With Illustrations.

"An intensely interesting little book. 'Our Joe' is a remarkable life-like picture, and the whole story abounds in those thrilling and pathetic passages which have made all the works of this author so deservedly popular. It is a striking and effective story, and will, if we mistake not, rank as one of the best of Mr. Hocking's less pretentious productions."—*Spalding Free Press.*

"It is a pathetic story, simply and effectively told."—*Edinburgh Daily Review.*

POOR MIKE:

The Story of a Waif.

"A little story fitted by its deep pathos less for children than for older folk."—*St. James's Gazette.*

"A very touching instance of cheerful, uncomplaining poverty."—*Watchman.*

"A very pathetic story of a waif."—*Yorkshire Post.*

"The book is thoroughly wholesome, and one which any parent may be glad to see in the hands of his son."—*Derby Mercury.*

"A more touching story could not well be penned."—*Edinburgh Daily Review.*

"The story is told by the author in a plaintive and natural way."—*Chester Courant.*

CHIPS:

A Story of Manchester Life.

Original Illustrations.

"Well adapted for circulation amongst Sunday-school children."—*Manchester Courier.*

"Nicely got up, illustrated, and tastefully bound."—*Preston Guardian.*

"Both young and old will feel a pleasure in its perusal."—*Burnley Express.*

"The good which such a story as this is calculated to effect cannot be estimated."—*Edinburgh Daily Review.*

"An interesting moral story, suitable for boys and girls."—*Halifax Courier.*

"The tale is interesting and the moral is satisfactory."—*Stamford Mercury.*

4

MEMOIR OF MRS. WAKEFIELD,

LATE WIFE OF REV. THOMAS WAKEFIELD, MISSIONARY TO EAST AFRICA.

BY THE REV. R. BREWIN.

Crown 8vo. *Illustrations.* Handsomely bound cloth, gilt edges, 3s. 6d.

"Rarely has a more touching story been offered to the public."--*Leeds Mercury.*

"Whoever begins it must read it right through."—*Wesleyan Methodist Magazine.*

"We must save this book for an article, for it is too full of interest to be dismissed with a few words."—C. H. SPURGEON, in *Sword and Trowel.*

"Mrs. Wakefield was a choice woman. . . . The scenes of the loss of her child and of her own illness are very touchingly told, and have made the reading of the memoir quite a means of grace to us."—C. H. SPURGEON Article in *Sword and Trowel.*

NORAH LANG, THE MINE GIRL.

By SALOME HOCKING.

Author of "Granny's Hero," "Fortunes of Riverside," &c.

With Original Illustrations.

Crown 8vo, cloth, gilt lettered, 1*s.* 6*d.* ; ditto, gilt edges, 2*s.*

"'Norah Lang' I have read through with unabated interest."—R. ABER-
CROMBIE, M.A.

"Miss Hocking has put into this story a large amount of entertaining
narrative, thrilling fact and startling adventure.—*New Connexion Magazine.*

"A delightful little book."—*Spalding Free Press.*

"A capital story well told."—*Lambeth Post.*

"An interesting story of village life . . . in which there is much sweet
sympathy and tenderness."—*Southport Guardian.*

In the Press.—THE

MINISTER OF EBENEZER CHAPEL.

A Story of Methodist Church Life.

By ANNIE M. BARTON. Author of "Agatha's Charge,"
"A Mysterious Way," &c. *With Original Illustrations.*
Crown 8vo, cloth gilt, gilt edges, 2*s.* 6*d.*

HARRY PENHALE : THE TRIAL OF HIS FAITH.

A Story for Young Men.

By JOSEPH HOCKING.

With Original Illustrations.

Crown 8vo, cloth gilt, gilt edges, 2s. 6d.

DADO;

Or, Stories of Native Life in East Africa.

By REV. W. YATES. *Illustrated.* Cloth, gilt lettered, 1s.

Suitable for a Missionary Reward.

"Full of interest."—*On the Road.*
"As instructive as it is interesting."—*Spalding Free Press.*
"Mr. Yates writes in a forcible and dramatic style."—R. ABERCROMBIE, M.A.

THE MARTYRS OF GOLBANTI;

Or, The Life and Labours of the Rev. John Houghton and his Heroic Wife.

By Rev. R. BREWIN.

Illustrated. Cloth, gilt lettered, 1s.

THE REV. J. HOUGHTON, OF GOLBANTI.

"A touching and thrilling narrative."—*The Spalding Free Press.*

"Mr. Brewin is a good writer. He has a simple and attractive style . . I have great pleasure in commending to the notice of our readers ' The Martyrs of Golbanti.' "—*Methodist Free Church Magazine.*

"The whole series are about the best got up we have seen."—*On the Road.*

10

In the Press.

THE CHRONICLES OF A QUIET FAMILY.

BY SALOME HOCKING.

Author of "Granny's Hero," "Norah Lang, the Mine Girl," &c., &c.

With Original Illustrations. Cloth, gilt lettered, 1s.

SEPTEM IN UNO:

Or, the First Seven Volumes of the Homilist in One.

BY DR. DAVID THOMAS.

Consisting of Germs of Thought, Leading Homilies, &c., &c.

Demy 8vo, cloth, gilt lettered, 12*s.* 6*d.*

The following are a few of the many testimonials to the value of the Homilist.—

The late Professor FINNEY—"Of unspeakable value."

GEORGE GILFILLAN, D.D.—"What Arnold would have loved, and Coleridge promised to contribute to. Altogether I never had more pleasure in reading and recommending. *O si sic omnia.*"

Dr. LANGE—"The best book published in England for the promotion pulpit oratory."

FREE METHODIST HAND-BOOK.

An Enlarged and Improved Edition.

BY W. BOYDEN AND E. ASKEW.

Cognizance is taken in various ways of the Jubilee of the Wesleyan Methodist Association, and the Silver Wedding of the United Methodist Free Churches.

Crown 8vo. 270 pp., cloth; gilt lettered, 3*s.*

"A repertory of information . . . carefully prepared . . . and perfectly reliable."—*The Primitive Methodist.*

"The silent representative of an immense amount of labour, time, patience, and painstaking . . . Every official member of our community ought to possess a copy.—*Methodist Free Church Magazine.*

CHOICE READINGS FOR LEISURE MOMENTS.

BY JACKSON WRAY.

Demy 8vo, cloth, gilt lettered, 548 pages, 2*s.* 6*d.*

A suitable present for a local preacher or Sunday-school teacher.

HOLIDAY RAMBLES

In England, Ireland, Scotland, and Wales.

Being a popular description of some of the most lovely Scenery, Ruins, and Places of Resort, &c., in the United Kingdom. Profusely Illustrated by some of our best Artists.

Price 2*s.*, Cloth Boards ; or Cloth Extra, Gilt Edges, 2*s.* 6*d.*

WILLIAM GRIFFITH:

Memorials and Letters.

By RICHARD CHEW.

Crown 8vo, with Steel Portrait, cloth, gilt lettered, 2s.; cloth extra, gilt edges, 2s. 6d.

"Mr. Chew has done the work he proposed carefully and well."—*Leeds Mercury*.

"The portrait is true to life, and admirably executed."—*Primitive Methodist Magazine*.

"A very readable and enjoyable book."—*The Free Methodist*.

A Cheap Edition, paper covers, crown 8vo, 1s.

HISTORIC SKETCHES OF FREE METHODISM.

By JOSEPH KIRSOP.

Cloth boards, 1s. 6d.; cloth extra, 2s.

"A useful handbook of information concerning the Free Churches of Methodism."—*Literary World*.

WORK WELL DONE:

Exemplified in the Life of the Rev. Robert Bushell.

By THE REV. S. S. BARTON.

Foolscap 8vo, with Portrait, gilt lettered, 1s. 6d.; cloth, without Portrait, 1s. 4d.; cloth limp, 1s.

GOSPEL SERMONS FOR CHILDREN.

By THE REV. R. BREWIN.

Crown 8vo, cloth, gilt lettered, 1s. 6d.

"Models of what sermons for children ought to be."—*Lambeth Post*.

"The author has a decided gift for teaching children the great truths of the gospel."—R. ABERCROMBIE, M.A.

13

MARRIAGE AND HOME LIFE.
By Dr. TALMAGE.
Crown 8vo, cloth gilt, bevelled boards, gilt edges, 2s. 6d.

FROM LOG CABIN TO WHITE HOUSE.
The Story of President Garfield's Life.
By WILLIAM M. THAYER.
Crown 8vo, cloth, gilt lettered. 348 pages, 2s. 6d.

TRUE NOBILITY;
Or, The Golden Deeds of an Earnest Life.
Being a Record of the Life of the late Earl of Shaftesbury.
By Dr. KIRTON.
Author of "Buy Your Own Cherries," &c.
Crown 8vo, cloth, gilt lettered, gilt edges. 425 pages, 2s. 6d.

MY MISSION GARDEN.
By the Rev. S. LANGDON.
Author of "Punchi Nona."
Crown 8vo, cloth gilt, bevelled boards, gilt edges, 2s. 6d.

LIFE AMONG THE MASSES.
Indicated in a Series of Touching Stories, Lectures, and Sermons.
By JOHN GUTTRIDGE.
Crown 8vo, cloth, gilt lettered. 392 pages, 2s. 6d. net.

JOHN RUSKIN.
His Life and Teaching.
By J. MARSHALL MATHER.
Second Edition, crown 8vo, cloth, 2s. 6d.

THE VILLAGE BLACKSMITH;
Or, The Life of Samuel Hick.
By JAMES EVERETT.
46,000. Crown 8vo, cloth, 2s. 6d.